Can We Talk?

Conversations About Mental
Health and Behaviors in Schools

Can We Talk?

Conversations About Mental Health and Behaviors in Schools

Kimberly K. Davis, Ed.D.

Top Performance Leadership Group, LLC

©2020 Kimberly K. Davis. All Rights Reserved.

9781716776427

About the Author

Dr. Kimberly Davis, Founder and Principal of Top Performance Leadership Group, LLC, is an Educational Leadership graduate in Transformational Leadership from Concordia University-Portland. Her research in Organization Development explored how practitioners of Appreciative Inquiry (AI) determine impact. She has identified a pivotal point in motivation to change; a key concept she has termed *the Paradigm Fulcrum*© (PF). The PF is an emerging concept she continues to develop by integrating Transformative Emotional Intelligence (TEI) with the strengths-based AI change model for coaching and training excellence in education, business, healthcare, and personal development. Dr. Davis is a successful speaker, entrepreneur, and business consultant, served as a business leader for major corporations, and is a published curriculum author. Dr. Davis served three years as a public-school district administrator as the Special Education Director while speaking, publishing, coaching, and consulting for business and educational organizations. She is further credentialed as a certified Appreciative Inquiry Facilitator, a certified Transformative Emotional Intelligence (TEI) coach, and Mental Health First Aid Trainer.

Table of Contents

FORWARD IX
PREFACE XI
INTRODUCTION XIII
CHAPTER 1: MENTAL HEALTH IN SCHOOLS 1
    YOUTH MENTAL HEALTH IN SCHOOLS 2
    MENTAL HEALTH DESCRIPTIONS 4
        Attention Deficit Hyperactive Disorder (ADHD) 5
        Autism Spectrum Disorder (ASD) 6
        Oppositional Defiant Disorder (ODD) 7
        Conduct Disorder (CD) 8
        Disruptive Mood Dysregulation Disorder (DMDD) 9
        Reactive Attachment Disorder (RAD) and Disinhibited Social Engagement Disorder (DSED) 9
    CHAPTER 1 SUMMARY 10
CHAPTER 2: TYPES OF BEHAVIORS 11
    FREQUENCY OF BEHAVIOR 12
    DURATION OF BEHAVIOR 13
    INTENSITY OF BEHAVIOR 13
    TIER 1 BEHAVIOR SUPPORT 14
    TIER 2 BEHAVIOR SUPPORT 14
    TIER 3 BEHAVIOR INTERVENTIONS 14
    TIER 4 BEHAVIOR SUPPORTS 15
    BEHAVIOR TYPE I – SITUATIONAL BEHAVIOR 16
    BEHAVIOR TYPE II – EPISODIC BEHAVIOR 17
    BEHAVIOR TYPE III - CHRONIC BEHAVIOR 17
    BEHAVIOR TYPE IV – MENTAL HEALTH DISORDER 18
    UNINTENDED CONSEQUENCES OF UNRESOLVED BEHAVIOR 19
    CHAPTER 2 SUMMARY 20
CHAPTER 3: ADDRESSING THE NEEDS OF YOUTH WITH MENTAL HEALTH AND BEHAVIOR DISORDERS 21
    EQUITY -VS- EQUALITY IN EDUCATION 22
    THE 504 PLAN 23
    AMERICANS WITH DISABILITIES AMENDMENTS 24
    QUALIFYING FOR A 504 PLAN 25
    INDIVIDUAL EDUCATION PLAN (IEP) 26
    ACCOMMODATIONS -VS- MODIFICATIONS 28
    EDUCATIONAL SETTINGS (PLACEMENT) 30
    GENERAL EDUCATION SETTING 32

    CO-TEACHING OR INCLUSION SETTING 32
        Resource Setting..33
        Self-Contained Setting..33
        Alternate Learning Environment (ALE) Setting......................34
            Therapeutic Day Treatment (TDT) Setting 34
            Residential Setting..34
    BEHAVIOR INTERVENTION PLAN (BIP) 35
    CONTENT OF A BEHAVIOR INTERVENTION PLAN 37
    COGNITIVE BEHAVIOR INTERVENTION 38
    MULTI-TIERED SYSTEMS OF SUPPORT (MTSS) 41
    DAVIS PERFORMANCE MODEL 43
        Situational Behavior..44
        Episodic Behavior 44
        Chronic Behavior 45
        Mental Illness or Disorder 46
        Key Takeaways of the Davis Performance Model....................46

CHAPTER 4: TEACHER SUPPORT AND TRAINING ON MENTAL HEALTH AND BEHAVIOR..51

    EDUCATOR ATTRITION AND BURNOUT 51
    EDUCATOR PREPARATION, DEVELOPMENT, AND SUPPORT 52
        Teacher Support 53
        Licensing Preparation and Professional Development............53
        Classroom Management Support..55
        District and Campus Discipline Policy Support 56

CHAPTER 5: INTEGRATING SUPPORTS FOR ADDRESSING MENTAL HEALTH ISSUES AND PROBLEMATIC STUDENT BEHAVIORS 59

    COGNITIVE BEHAVIOR THEORY 60
    POSITIVE BEHAVIOR INTERVENTIONS AND SUPPORTS (PBIS) 60
    WHOLE SCHOOL, WHOLE COMMUNITY, WHOLE CHILD MODEL 61
    INTEGRATED LEARNING 61
    SCHOOL BASED MENTAL HEALTH PROGRAMS (SBMH).............63
    MENTAL HEALTH FIRST AID (MHFA) 64
    BEHAVIOR MANAGEMENT TRAINING 65
    CHAPTER 5 SUMMARY 66

CHAPTER 6: SOLUTIONS FOR SCHOOLS SUPPORTING MENTAL HEALTH AND BEHAVIOR..67

    EDUCATIONAL REFORM TO SUPPORT MENTAL HEALTH AND BEHAVIOR IN SCHOOLS 67

REFORM TEACHER SUPPORT AND TRAINING 67
THE TEACHER DEVELOPMENT BOOK STUDY: SEL/TEI FOR K-12
EDUCATORS..69
REFORM STUDENT SUPPORTS FOR MENTAL HEALTH AND BEHAVIOR
74
REFORM DISCIPLINE SUPPORTS FOR MENTAL HEALTH AND
BEHAVIOR 75
REFORM SCHOOL SAFETY PLANS FOR MENTAL HEALTH AND
BEHAVIOR AWARENESS AND PROACTIVE STRATEGIES 76
TALK ABOUT IT! 77

REFERENCES..**79**

Forward

It is a distinct privilege and pleasure to construct the Foreword for the to-the-point book *Can We Talk? Conversations About Mental Health and Behaviors in Schools*. For many years there has been growing need to begin talks and meaningful, holistic dialogue about mental health and behaviors generally, and especially in our public schools. Facilitated through this pointed book, we now have a new beginning point for conversations that will provide positive and specific focus to address a growing crisis for schools, teachers, administrators, and families; everyone, really, who is involved with the welfare of our children. Dr. Kimberly Davis has opened the door for this dialogue to take place immediately.

I know Dr. Davis and have seen first-hand her excellent work in education, business, government, and career/life environments. As a current special education director and former classroom teacher in public schools, she has unique and supportive training, experience, and skills through her certifications in all core content areas, special education, English as a second language, school administration, appreciative inquiry, emotional intelligence, and as a mental health first aid trainer with an earned doctorate in education and transformational leadership. Through continuing graduate studies with the University of Arkansas, she will soon add her BCBA (behavior analyst) certification to this impressive list. As such, she has a rare combination of ability and insight into child mental health and how current efforts fall far short of achieving the mental, behavioral, and achievement goals needed within schools, school districts, and education systems locally, nationally, and globally.

Clearly, there is a need to be mindful of policies and responsible actions regarding the whole child and at all levels (from pre-K through12 and beyond) to develop successful, responsible citizens, one child at a time, and to holistically include every child. With this responsibility, there has been and continues to be a trend of top-down policy which is good in many ways. And yet, this *one-size-fits-all* style simply does not work as intended for each child, family, teachers, and the education community. All of us are affected by mental and behavioral challenges that create disruption and issues in the classroom and treatment facilities. This book provides a basis for more capably discussing, addressing, and meeting these challenges.

As a psychologist and educator, I have noted discussions and conversations about mental, behavioral, and emotional health that were not constructive or helpful. Dr. Davis understands the need for research, data collection plans, and evidence-based approaches essential to creating pathways to solutions that work. One of her gifts is to create constructive, positive, and realistic projects that work for teachers, families, schools, students, and their communities.

This is a must-read book to begin reforms necessary for our children now that will reap societal benefits well into the future. Yes, Let's Talk . . . and take prudent actions.

Gary R. Low, Ph.D.

Professor Emeritus of Education, Texas A&M University-Kingsville

Founding Faculty, Emotional Intelligence Training & Research Institute

Co-author, Teaching and Learning Excellence and the Emotional Learning System

Preface

The public-school landscape is changing rapidly with two complimentary phenomena fueling negative growth patterns in school violence, suicide rates, and other behavioral problems. The first phenomenon is a marked increase in the number of students with some form of mental health or behavior disorder. Support for Social and Emotional Learning (SEL) in schools has been led by The Collaborative for Academic, Social, and Emotional Learning (CASEL) which, more than two decades ago, collaborated with the Illinois State Board of Education and Illinois Children's Mental Health Partnership to develop SEL standards, goals, and age-appropriate benchmarks and performance descriptors, all facilitated through the Children's Mental Health Act of 2003. More recently, support for SEL in K-12 education has grown through specific provisions of the Every Student Succeeds Act (Sean Grant et al., 2017). Additionally, positive education has been shown to increase academic performance and overall happiness (Seligman et al., 2009). However, although these steps hold promise, they do not sufficiently or explicitly address the issue of students with mental health or behavior disorders, a problem noted each year with increasing frequency in the public-schools. A second problematic phenomenon is an alarming attrition rate of teachers from Pre-Kindergarten through 12th grades. According to a Learning Policy Report (Carver-Thomas & Darling-Hammond, 2017) there is an 8% annual attrition rate nationwide with the number of teachers leaving the profession comprising up to 90% of the annual demand. Teacher frustration and burnout are stoked by discipline problems and low student motivation (Skaalvik & Skaalvik, 2017), both of which are influenced by mental health and behavior disorders. This book was influenced by a recent study of teacher development in emotional intelligence skills to help reduce stress and burnout by integrating SEL into pedagogical practices and better prepare teachers and administrators to support the needs of students with mental health and behavior disorders. Initial observations from this study are presented in Chapter 6.

Introduction

Think back to helpful conversations you have had about mental health and behavior in schools. In my experience there hasn't been much consensus on how to help schools deal effectively with this challenge. Within these pages is information about the current status of mental health amongst our youth and a brief description of some of the most common, yet severe, mental health and behavior disorders we see in our schools. Following the brief mental health discussion is my strategy and intervention planning framework for districts and campuses. This book includes an overview of the ways students diagnosed with mental health or behavior disorders are served and taught, as well as a summary of foundational theories to support current trends of integrated learning environments. The final chapter is an outline of solutions that need to be brought to the discussion and addresses education preparation, training and support, student early intervention and in-school support, discipline that works, and safety planning considerations. Though this book provides a crosswalk across district practices and opportunities to reform educational practices through the Every Student Succeeds Act, it is not intended to be an all-inclusive handbook or exhaustive of all resources. Rather, it is an outline to guide the hard conversations that need to happen with a framework to plan new ways of delivering education that is inclusive, meaningful, and effective. The purpose of this book is to talk about it!

Chapter 1: Mental Health in Schools

Leading a school district's Special Education Department, it is easy to witness the span of behaviors across the grade levels. Having served students with special needs over the past decade and across two states, the change in students attending public schools has become alarming. As I attend regional leadership conferences and training there is much discussion around the concerns for the number of students with extreme, unresolved or chronic mental health and behavior disorders. That means they have extreme emotional and physical outbursts over triggers that would not warrant that level of reaction in students who are ready to learn.

I want to take a moment to discuss how I look at student behaviors and will expand this discussion in later chapters. To keep the support level consistent with the standard Tier system used for academic Response to Intervention (RtI) (National Center for Learning Disabilities, 2019), I will begin with a three-tiered description for behavior supports. This convention will make it easier to build these supports into your current campus plans. The first level of behavior support, Tier 1, is focused in the classroom in the same way that Tier 1 academic interventions are focused. This level of support focuses on the teacher's classroom management skills regarding students who experience an occasional upset to their emotional balance. Tier 2 support would include some sort of pull out or other outside-of-classroom support. Tier 2 supports could be a counselor or therapist that pulls the student for services, or a planned intervention time where students work on social-emotional learning or growth mindset types of instructional programming. Tier 3 behavior support would be more specific to chronic and problematic issues that interfere with the student's access to the general education curriculum or interferes with their peer's access to learning. Tier 3 approaches may include an Alternate Learning Environment (ALE) classroom that could be utilized to support the student in a reduced class size to facilitate the child's transition back into the general education setting. In addition to Tiers 1-3, I am advocating for a fourth tier that would be a more intense and structured environment for those students with chronic and extreme emotional dysregulation. With the prevalence of childhood mental illness, changes in options available to support the needs of these students, and our requirement to provide a Free and Appropriate Public Education (FAPE), now is the time to engage in conversations about relevant educational reforms to meet this population's needs, protect their peers and teachers, and help them become productive, self-evident, and independent members of our society.

Youth Mental Health in Schools

Mental disorders among youth are described as serious changes in the way children typically learn, behave, or handle their emotions, causing distress and problems getting through the day (Danielson et al., 2018). The

National Council for Behavioral Health (2016) further defined a mental disorder or mental illness as "a diagnosable illness that affects a person's thinking, emotional state, and behavior as well as disrupts the person's ability to work or carry out other daily activities and engage in satisfying personal relationships" (p. 4) The most prevalent health issue in school-aged children is mental health disorders. One in five children suffers from a mental health or learning disorder that causes some degree of impairment, and up to 90% of chronic mental disorders begin in early childhood (Child Mind Institute, 2016; Mayo Clinic, 2020; "Mental health disorders in adolescents," 2017). What is more alarming is that one in 10 youth has a disorder that causes significant impairment ("Mental Health Disorders in Adolescents," 2017).

> 1 in 10 youth has a mental disorder that causes significant impairment to their learning or the learning of their peers.

　　　In 2016, the Child Mind Institute published their annual report with the theme related to school-based needs and long-term outcomes. This issue emphasized the poor outcomes in school and life for children that suffer mental health and learning disorders. The report also advocated for updated discipline approaches to avoid increasing the likelihood of impeding student's chances of success. What is needed is "A widely deployed, integrated system of evidence-supported, school-based mental health and preventive services" (Child Mind Institute, 2016). The report investigated the negative effects of mental health disorders in school, early intervention and prevention programs, and school-wide behavior plans and targeted interventions.

Mental Health Descriptions

The following descriptions are intended as a brief overview of the mental health disorders seen in our public schools. The information is not intended to be all inclusive, or applicable to all students with behavioral disorders or even to suggest that a student with a particular diagnosis would exhibit all of these symptoms. Rather it is an attempt to bring awareness to the social-emotional-educational needs that youth with these disorders may have and, through that awareness, help develop empathy, strategize early intervention, and create success plans within the school setting. Though you will hear it stated throughout the discussion that a youth may have any of these disorders on a continuum of severity, they may also, and frequently do, have a combination of more than one disorder. It is generally understood that when a diagnosis is determined, there may be comorbidity, or additional mental disorders (Krueger, 1999; Linke et al., 2020; Nobel et al., 2020; Wichstrøm et al., 2019). These descriptions are not intended for school personnel to diagnose or recommend treatment for students. Again, the purpose is to introduce key concepts and to open a dialogue among education professionals, families, community members, and policy makers to inform better behavior supports, understanding, educator preparation and training, and campus and district structures to better serve students in public school settings.

Attention Deficit Hyperactive Disorder (ADHD)

Attention Deficit Hyperactive Disorder (ADHD) has been thought of in education as an information processing disorder. ADHD is one of the most commonly identified disabilities served under an Individual Education Plan (IEP) through the Individuals with Disabilities in Education Act (IDEA) or under Section 504 of the Americans with Disabilities Act (ADA) (i.e., a 504 plan).

The Diagnostic and Statistical Manual of Mental Disorders defined ADHD as a persistent condition that impairs functioning or development, and characterized by chronic inattention, hyperactivity, and often impulsivity (American Psychiatric Association, 2013). Millions of children are diagnosed with ADHD annually, some as early as three years of age but usually identified by the onset of adolescence. It is more common in boys than girls and though people may learn effective coping strategies, it is often something they will have to manage into adulthood.

Unfortunately, ADHD can be somewhat debilitating in school aged children causing students to struggle academically, be prone to more accidents, suffer with self-esteem, have difficulty with relationships, and have an increased risk of delinquent behaviors such as substance abuse or other illegal activities. Another compounding concern of having ADHD is the possibility of coexisting conditions that are frequently present in children and can further impede their learning and social development. Though these additional disorders are frequently seen in children with ADHD, they are not caused by it, but they do severely complicate the condition. Common coexisting psychological or developmental conditions related to ADHD include Oppositional Defiant Disorder (ODD), Conduct Disorder, Disruptive Mood Dysregulation Disorder, learning disabilities, substance abuse disorders, anxiety disorders, mood disorders, Autism Spectrum Disorder (ASD), and Tic Disorder or Tourette Syndrome. Any one of these coexisting conditions can cause interruptions in the typical development of a child academically, socially, or emotionally. When suffered in plural, the combination of these challenges will likely be significantly debilitating to children and often present as a mental health or behavior disorder.

Autism Spectrum Disorder (ASD)

Autism Spectrum Disorder (ASD) has a relatively new framework under the DSM-5. Under the previous version diagnostic manual individuals could be diagnosed with four separate disorders: Autistic Disorder, Asperger's Disorder, Childhood Disintegrative Disorder, or the catch-all diagnosis of Pervasive Developmental Disorder not otherwise specified. Due to inconsistencies in diagnostic practices, researchers redefined ASD for more consistent and accurate diagnostic criteria. As described in the DSM-5, individuals identified with traits of, or diagnosed with, ASD often suffer communication deficits, such as responding inappropriately in conversations, misreading nonverbal interactions, or having difficulty building friendships appropriate to their age. Additionally, they may be overly dependent on routines, highly sensitive to changes in their environment, or intensely focused on inappropriate items. It is important to note that symptoms exhibited by people with ASD fall on a continuum, with some individuals showing mild symptoms and others having much more severe symptoms. The spectrum continuum provides a basis for the variations in symptoms and behaviors between individuals.

Part of the DSM-5 criteria requires individuals to show symptoms from early childhood, even if those symptoms are not actually identified until later in life. The change in criteria allows for an earlier diagnosis while allowing those whose symptoms may not be identified until social demands exceed their capacity to receive the diagnosis.

Oppositional Defiant Disorder (ODD)

The American Academy of Child and Adolescent Psychiatry (2019) described Oppositional Defiant Disorder (ODD) As a condition of oppositional and uncooperative behavior that exists beyond toddler age as an ongoing pattern of uncooperative, defiant, and hostile behavior toward authority figures that seriously interferes with the child's day-to-day functioning. Symptoms may include frequent temper tantrums, excessive arguing with adults, questioning of rules, active defiance and refusal to comply with adult requests and rules, deliberate attempts to annoy or upset people, blaming others for their mistakes or misbehavior, often being touchy or easily annoyed by others, frequent anger and resentment, mean and hateful talking when upset, and/or spiteful attitude and revenge seeking. the symptoms can be seen across all settings but are most likely to be seen at home or school. Up to 16% of all school-aged students have ODD and may be influenced by biological, psychosocial, and social factors.

Conduct Disorder (CD)

Conduct Disorder (CD) is actually a term used to describe a group of repetitive and persistent behavioral and emotional problems in children. Children in this category generally have difficulty following rules, respecting the rights of others, showing empathy, and behaving in a socially acceptable way. Some of the behaviors that may be exhibited by individuals suffering from CD may include aggression towards animals and people in the following ways: bullies, threatens or intimidates others, delights in being cruel or mean to others, starts physical fights, has used a weapon that could cause serious physical harm to others, is physically cruel to people or animals, steals from a victim while hurting them, forces someone into sexual activity, shows no genuine remorse after an aggressive episode, deliberately engages in fire setting with the intention to cause damage, deliberately destroys others' property, has broken into someone else's personal property, lies to obtain goods, or favors or to avoid obligations, steals items without confronting a victim as would be seen in shoplifting, and any other serious violations of rules

(American Academy of Child and Adolescent Psychiatry, 2018).

Disruptive Mood Dysregulation Disorder (DMDD)

The DSM – 5 Describes Disruptive Mood Dysregulation Disorder (DMDD) As a condition that exhibits as severe, recurrent temper outbursts manifested verbally and or behaviorally that are grossly out of proportion in intensity or duration to the situation or provocation. The temper outbursts are inconsistent with developmental level and can occur, on average, three or more times per week. the mood between temper outbursts is persistently irritable or angry most of the day, nearly every day, and is observable by others (American Psychiatric Association, 2013).

Reactive Attachment Disorder (RAD) and Disinhibited Social Engagement Disorder (DSED)

Reactive Attachment Disorder (RAD) and Disinhibited Social Engagement Disorder (DSED) are classified as stressor-related disorders that result from social neglect. The two terms are similar except DSED presents with externalizing behavior making a child readily interact with unfamiliar adults as opposed to internalizing behavior and being more withdrawn and depressive (American Psychiatric Association, 2013). There have been numerous studies over the decades to substantiate the need for social bonding and attachment in infants as a means for typical emotional and mental development. What may be an unintended consequence of technology advances is the use of electronic devices as a means to pacify young children in stores, car rides, during busy times at home (cooking, talking on the phone, working from home, etc.) or in lieu of actual books and the changes in brain development with excessive screen time. As a society, we may be inadvertently causing these detachment disorders not through gross neglect and child maltreatment, but rather through providing too much screen time to children under the age of five (Hutton et al., 2019). There are also interruptions to the positive social interactions when an electronic device is used with the child over an actual book. This may be evidenced in one study where "toddlers and parents engaged in more frequent social control behaviors and less social reciprocity when reading tablet-based vs print books" (Munzer et al., 2019). Clearly, continued research is needed.

Chapter 1 Summary

This chapter is an introduction to some of the types of mental health disorders occurring at a rate of up to 20% of our total student population (Mental Health First Aid USA, 2020). One in five students will be diagnosed with a mental health or behavior disorder of some type that interrupts their education and can cause the disruption of peer education, the formation of healthy relationships, and presents unique school safety concerns. As the mental health landscape for children continues to evolve, I and other researchers recommend continued research into contemporary cultural factors that may be contributing to the behavioral changes we are seeing in our children.

Chapter 2: Types of Behaviors

I want to start the discussion of the behaviors seen in schools with the idea that all children act out sometimes and that is a normal phenomenon. I also want to emphasize that if a child does act out, it does not mean they suffer a mental disorder of some sort. There are also children who suffer mental disorders that do not act out. So, I want you to keep an open mind to the wide range of behavioral aspects of normal childhood development. Children have free will and the exploration of boundaries is a rite of passage for a typically developing child. Behavioral challenges, therefore, are not always the result of mental disorders nor even necessarily a parenting issue. At the same time, we are witnessing behavioral challenges in schools today that were not seen at the current frequency in previous decades.

My goal is to encourage discussions of the types of behavior seen in schools in order to create a space to acknowledge the level of support a student and teacher may need as we help the child learn to cope within their environment. Merely manipulating the environment to help youth cope does not work, teach self-efficacy, or independence. However, each person, and each environment will be a unique situation and caution should be used when applying a blanket assumption to an individual scenario. In the span of this discussion, I divide behavior into four types and give a description of each that is based on parameters of frequency, duration, and intensity. Often supporting mental health and behavior needs within a school setting is done through special services (a special education plan or 504 plan) with supports and goal tracking recorded for academic achievement and skill acquisition. Many times, implementation and achievement is documented through frequency, duration, and intensity with the construction of goals and objectives in those plans. In the scope of this discussion, I will also identify the intervention Tier and educational setting that may be used to support student behavior by level. In the following chapter, I will describe serving the mental health and behavior needs of students in a public school through, behavior management training, special programing, and behavior intervention planning. Before I describe the Types of behaviors, I will identify the parameters used in this discussion for frequency, duration, and intensity.

Frequency of Behavior

The frequency of behavior is a strong contributor to the identification of the Type and Tier that should be used to support the student as well as the educational setting that could be employed. When a student has a behavior that exhibits infrequently, meaning less than two times per week or sporadically and may present as occasional occurrences. Frequent behavior will be described as occurring two to three times per week or may recur over a prolonged period. Frequent behavior may happen over a number of consecutive days or intermittently over a longer time period. Behavior may be considered severe if the behavior happens more than three times per week or is pervasive in the student's day or across all settings.

Duration of Behavior

Duration refers to how long the behavior lasts. Short term behavior may last a few moments to a few hours but would be described in this discussion as an event that would last less than a day, as a general rule. Long term durations are characterized as recurring short-term behaviors that repeat frequently and may continue for an extended period (up to six months). Duration may be described as pervasive when it is seen in the student throughout their day and across all settings.

Intensity of Behavior

Intensity of behavior can range from mild as might be seen in students from an autonomic, emotional reaction to not getting their way, or when they are tired or hungry and feeling 'grouchy' to full on tantrums. More severe behavior may result in destruction of property or attempts to harm self or others. What has become more prevalent is the increase in the intensity of behaviors that cross all ages and grade levels. Better training in recognizing the physical and emotional changes in an individual as they are escalating to implement proper supports is paramount to helping these students learn to cope with their environment and prevent severe behavior outbursts.

Tier 1 Behavior Support

Tier one behavior support is generally identified as basic classroom management skills. This support goes beyond the rules and regulations for the school or classroom. Tier one supports are the classroom procedures and de-escalation techniques used to teach a child to be self-aware and learn to self-regulate. There may be some need to enlist the additional support of a team teacher or an administrator, sometimes but the majority of Tier one support should happen by the teacher and between the teacher and parent, in partnership with one another.

Tier 2 Behavior Support

Tier 2 behavior support will include Tier 1 interventions, as well as additional pull-out or push-in activities to help teach the child specific skills needed to be successful. These additional activities might be from the teacher, teaching team, administrator, school counselor, or a therapist within the district. As with Tier 1 interventions, the parents or caregiver should be included or invited as a partner in the structure for the student. Important to note is the flexibility between the levels of intervention Tiers and supports based on the need of the child. The overarching goal is to meet them where they are and provide the support necessary for them to learn self-regulation and find success in their day and subsequent life path.

Tier 3 Behavior Interventions

Tier 3 behavior supports encompass both Tiers 1 and 2 and should mirror the need of the student entering a chronic or crisis behavior. As the child escalates the behavior, the intervention level Tiers and support increase; as the child de-escalates, the behavior Tiers and support decrease. When a child enters the Tier 3 level of support, boundaries and expectations are placed until the student is able to regain control. As the student increases self-control adult control is gradually transferred back to the student. As an example, a student in Tier 3 support may have a tendency to run from the adults or attempt to leave the building or campus. The need to keep that student safe is more important than empowering them in that moment. In these moments, the adults will need to closely monitor the student while preventing their exit. As the child regains their self-control, or regulation, the guarding of the exits may no longer be necessary and the restriction of their movement around the building may be eased. A student who enters Tier 3 may be under a chronic and severe behavior classification and may need the support of medical professionals who can determine whether the student needs pharmaceutical interventions. A behavior intervention plan (BIP) may be helpful for these students with procedures in place by the district for how to construct and implement these supports.

Tier 4 Behavior Supports

Anyone can benefit from a Tier 4 behavior support should they enter an emotional crisis. This does not indicate a mental health issue unless the behaviors become chronic or pervasive and interfere routinely with their daily activities or learning, which may lead to a diagnosis of a mental health disorder. Tier 4 behavior supports may add changes in the educational setting, pharmaceutical interventions, or psychotherapy as prescribed by a mental health provider. If a child has frequent behavior that has duration and intensity a behavioral analysis should be done by a qualified professional and a behavior support plan should be developed. Some of the behavior plans may require a crisis plan be written and formalized for the student.

Behavior Type I – Situational Behavior

Situational behavior is a temporary condition and may be more accurately described as having a bad day. The child may be tired, hungry, or perceive having been slighted by a friend or family member; or maybe, they just got up on the wrong side of the bed, as the adage goes. What is important to note is the frequency, duration, and intensity when a child has these days. When these parameters are low, the child is not likely to need much support outside the humanistic empathy that might offer a sense of comfort in that moment of need. Classroom teachers, school leaders and staff, and parents should be attuned to these instances as opportunities to introduce social-emotional skill development into the conversation with the child. The goal of the conversation is to help the child identify how to process their feelings toward productive outcomes, including options to their current reactions when experiencing such feelings (i.e., teaching metacognition, self-awareness, and constructive thinking). Situational behaviors may be best supported in the classroom as a Tier 1 behavior and may also require a Tier

2 intervention from an administrator, school counselor or therapist, or a phone call home in some cases.

Behavior Type II – Episodic Behavior

Episodic behavior can be triggered by a situational experience, but the duration would be over a more extended time period. This type of behavior may be seen during times of divorce, extended illnesses or death, moving, parental remarriage, new siblings, changing grades or schools, etc. The important consideration for Episodic behavior is to find a way to help the student identify and articulate what they are struggling with so proper supports can be put in place. If unsupported and the duration continues for an extended time period, the behavior may change to a more Chronic behavior problem. Episodic behavior may benefit most from a Tier 2 intervention with a school counselor or therapist to help the student reframe their thoughts into a productive outcome. Grief is a normal emotion and should not be stifled or ignored. Teaching and learning more constructive ways of processing difficult feelings will lead to more healthy outcomes and life and school.

Behavior Type III - Chronic Behavior

Chronic behaviors are more generally a result of unresolved or poorly processed Episodic behaviors. These behaviors become chronic because the duration has become extended and the child has not learned a better coping strategy or the triggering event occurs over an extended period of time. Some examples may be grief that turns to depression, or a trauma that becomes Post Traumatic Stress Disorder (PTSD). Any emotional response that does not resolve within a reasonable amount of time into a constructive thought process increases the risk to becoming a chronic condition, regardless whether there is a predisposition to mental illness. However, having a mental disorder may increase the likelihood of a behavior enduring. Chronic behavior will require Tier 2 interventions to be established and could require a temporary Tier 3 support until the behavior is resolved.

Behavior Type IV – Mental Health Disorder

Mental health disorders can lead to behavior disorders for most individuals. Not that behavior dysregulation cannot happen in any of the other behavior types, but the frequency, duration, and intensity are the factors used to identify and establish educational goals and objectives for emotional dysregulation interventions. The myriad of possible mental disorders and the potential coexisting conditions can complicate the needs of the children and those they encounter and interact with during the day. Some children are predisposed to a tendency to develop these behaviors, some develop them over time based on their life experiences and environmental exposures, and some develop them over time because the lower need emotions and behaviors were not properly or adequately processed. Emotional dysregulation will likely require all Tier levels of support for students to learn how to navigate their social and emotional needs in a school environment. Tier 4 levels of support may include alternate settings as would be seen with a Therapeutic Day Treatment (TDT) or a Behavior Support Classroom (BSC) that helps the student move forward in constructive ways. The goal is to support the child's behavioral needs and encourage positive emotional development to achieve academic success through social-emotional integration.

Unintended Consequences of Unresolved Behavior

Many times, our students are left to their own devices to manage their own social and emotional development. As the child grows and reaches puberty the problem can become worse. Especially after reaching the middle school grades, when teachers only see them for a single class period per day and students are less likely to talk about their feelings with adults, they can be left to navigate their sometimes tumultuous social-emotional worlds with little more than their own internal compass. Identifying students who are in need has been a priority for schools in attempts to reduce school violence, gang activity, drug and alcohol use, and self-harm. By the time they reach middle school, however, it is much too late! As mentioned, up to 20% of our students have a mental health need by age six and up to 10% of our students will have a mental health need that will cause severe behavior by age six. Here is where I suggest we change our educational paradigm. Simply put, the new approach will require educators at all levels, and especially at the early childhood and elementary school levels, to be proactive and plan supports according to behavior Tiers and Types – before the need for crisis interventions.

Chapter 2 Summary

Chapter 2 is a discussion of how I view behavior in schools, as well as levels of tiered support needed to best serve students. I have described frequency, duration, and intensity as parameters for defining behavior and the supports that may be needed as well as four Tiers of support to match the student's emotional and physical needs during a behavior event. For this discussion, I have also presented a hierarchy of behavior classifications. Situational Behavior that is temporary as seen when tired or hungry; Episodic Behavior that could be caused by events such as divorce or death; Chronic Behavior that is longer in duration that may come from traumatic experience or prolonged and unresolved emotional responses (grief); and Mental Illness that may be caused, or complicated, by mental health disorders or pervasive chronic conditions.

Chapter 3: Addressing the Needs of Youth with Mental Health and Behavior Disorders

All students are mandated to attend school; it is compulsory. Students who have been identified with a disability are entitled to a *free appropriate public education* (FAPE) under federal law. This chapter will provide a brief overview of how students may be best served in a public-school setting. I will include a brief description of how some special services can be provided. This list is not intended to be all-inclusive or exhaustive, by any means, but provides a good place to start. There may also be slight variations in programming between states, or different requirements in other countries. Also, it is important to note that the accommodations, modifications, or related services offered can vary greatly between two students with the same qualifying disability because they are provided based on the individual need of the student, not as a one-size-fits-all under a specific diagnosis or qualifying disability. In this chapter I provide an overview of the 504 plan, the Individual Education Plan (IEP), and a Behavior Intervention Plan (BIP) as means for documenting accommodations and modifications for students. This chapter will also provide a short discussion of educational settings, or placements, that can offer different levels of support to students. The goal for this chapter is to integrate the information covered in Chapters 1 and 2 using accepted and widely used education tools to proactively design and implement needed supports.

Equity -vs- Equality in Education

I do not feel that I can begin a conversation about special services without first addressing the argument of equity versus equality in education. Equality is derived from the word equal, meaning everyone gets the same thing. Though having equality in education has a nice ring, and I generally hear that equality is what is *fair*, I must pause the conversation to clarify these important concepts.

Think about your own kids, or someone's kids you know. Even within the same household, children grow and reach milestones at different times. It will be heard, often, that a child will learn to walk, or talk, or feed themselves at different times – in their own time. We know that, accept that, and allow for that difference in children until they begin Kindergarten; then we expect them to all be the same. The fact is, they are not the same. I once saw a Facebook meme that said something like, *expecting all students to learn at the same rate and in the same way is like expecting them to all wear the same size clothes.* We all know people that have learned something faster, or slower, than ourselves. We can probably all think back to a time in school when we felt super smart, or not, because of something we were learning, or struggling to learn. These individual differences are what make us unique and interesting, and they are why equity in education is crucial. When properly conceptualized and implemented, equity in education helps ensure that each student gets what they *need* to be successful and accepts that each student needs something different. Equity in education is what differentiated instruction is all about. Differentiated instruction, therefore, should be common practice in every classroom.

Sometimes, however, a student needs more support than even differentiated instruction to find success in school. When this happens, special support and services can make education accessible by reducing problematic behavior. Please note that accommodations or modifications should be specific to the student's identified disability or *qualifying category*. For example, if a student has a math deficit as a qualifying category for Math Calculation, they may be given a calculator (depending on the age and severity) but would not need small group testing based on this single deficit.

The 504 Plan

Since 1990 the Americans with Disabilities Act (ADA) has afforded civil rights protections to individuals with disabilities similar to those provided to individuals based on race, gender, national origin, and religion. It guarantees equal opportunities for individuals with disabilities in employment, public accommodations, transportation, state and local government services, and telecommunications. The ADA Amendments Act of 2008 (Amendments Act) became effective January 1, 2009.

While it amended the 1990 law, it also contained an amendment to the Rehabilitation Act of 1973 (Rehabilitation Act), a principal component of which was the improved description of the term disability. Though the term *disability* was already being used in both laws, the Amendments Act required a more broadly interpreted definition. As a result, students who qualify for support services under Section 504 will have certain requirements of the district to meet their equitable educational needs, as well as document those services through a Section 504 educational plan (i.e., a 504 plan).

Americans with Disabilities Amendments

School districts that receive federal program money are subject to the ADA and Rehabilitation Act regulations, and they are required to protect the FAPE rights of their students. The changes under the Amendments Act may increase the number of 504 plans in the district as some students may have been previously served under a health plan through the nurse's office, but now qualify for academic support under Section 504. In the amendments, the definition of being *substantially limited* is restored and no longer requires the student to have a *significant* or *severe* restriction. Additionally, the amendments expanded the definition of *major life activities* so that a student only has to have an impairment of one major life activity in order to qualify for services. Another change is the requirement of districts to make eligibility determinations based on the student's disability as it presents *without* mitigating measures. What this means is the disability is determined without the consideration of whether they are wearing devices such as hearing aids, are prescribed medications, or have learned behavioral adaptations. The only exception to this amendment is ordinary eyeglasses or contact lenses. In other words, a person would not be eligible for a 504 plan because they needed to wear glasses or contact lenses. When a student uses a mitigating measure to gain equitable access to the general education curriculum, they cannot be excluded from services under a 504 plan. However, if the disability is *transitory and minor*, the student shall not be regarded as having a disability. The amendment defines transitory as an impairment with an actual or expected duration of 6 months or less.

Qualifying for a 504 Plan

The purpose of Section 504 of the Rehabilitation Act of 1973 is to protect the rights of individuals with disabilities in programs and activities that receive federal funding for their entity. Schools receive federal funds and are, therefore, subject to the regulations. Under the 1990 amendments, course grades, when considered alone, are not a qualifying basis to determine an impairment and in need of support under a 504 plan. Additionally, having a medical diagnosis is not an automatic qualifying factor for 504 services, either. In order to qualify for a 504 plan a student must have a physical or mental impairment that substantially limits one or more major life activities, or have a record of such impairment, or be regarded as having such an impairment, regardless of the severity. Each student is considered individually, on a case-by-case determination.

As mentioned, grades, alone, are not a qualifying factor for a student to receive support under a 504 plan. There are a variety of data sources used to evaluate, document and determine which services, if any, are needed. A committee of knowledgeable individuals (licensed school personnel) must meet to review the collected data and make decisions about the student's educational needs. Parents are required to be notified of the committee and the decisions made, but their consent and participation are not required. I think it is important to note that most schools would have a policy to include the parent in the meetings and decisions even though it is not required. The 504 plans must have a "periodic" re-evaluation and annual review. The general provision is to follow the Individuals with Disabilities in Education Act (IDEA) guidelines for annual reviews of services and three-year re-evaluations for continued eligibility. There is, also, a requirement for re-evaluation before any significant change in placement can occur, which is any change in the educational setting for services. Educational settings are described later in this chapter. There is no provision under Section 504 that would require the school to incur the expense for an independent (outside of school) evaluation should the parent or guardian choose that route.

Individual Education Plan (IEP)

All students who are eligible for an Individual Education Plan (IEP) are eligible for a 504 plan, however, not all students eligible for a 504 plan will qualify for an IEP. There are 13 qualifying disabilities under an IEP. The categories include Autism, Blindness, Vision Impairment, Deafness, Hearing Impairment, Emotional Disturbance, Intellectual Disability, Orthopedic Impairment, Specific Learning Disability, Speech or Language Impairment, Traumatic Brain Injury, and Other Health Impairment. Once a referral to special education has been made and accepted, an IEP committee is formed that includes at least three members with the following five roles represented: Designee for the district, general education teacher, special education teacher, person qualified to interpret the student assessment data, and parent. The IEP and processes are governed by the Individuals with Disabilities Education Act (IDEA, 1990). The IDEA regulations ensure a student is entitled to and receives specific programming, supports, or class setting to best meet the needs of that particular student in the least restrictive environment, access to specialists through related services (i.e. – speech-language pathologists, occupational therapists, and physical therapists). Importantly, the law requires that supports are offered in the least restrictive environment.

The purpose of the IEP is to provide equitable access to the general education classroom that simultaneously meets the needs of a student with one of the qualifying disabilities. As mentioned earlier, having a learning difference or disability can span an entire spectrum of needs and severity, hence, the creation of an Individual Education Plan. The IDEA regulations are specific to how students qualify, having annual reviews of services, monitoring and reporting goal progress, and re-evaluating the student's eligibility every three years. While some related services may require annual assessments for Medicaid eligibility, the topic of Medicaid eligibility is outside the scope of this book.

Accommodations -vs- Modifications

It is important to think about how a student may be supported in the classroom. Supports are generally considered in terms of accommodations or modifications depending on a student's needs. Accommodations are differences in how we ask a student to do their work or demonstrate mastery that is on their grade level and at the same rigor of instruction as their non-disabled peers. In other words, a student with an IEP may be asked to complete 10 math questions instead of 20 questions if they can demonstrate knowledge in the shortened assignment. Another example could be a student who needs additional time to complete the 20 math questions, which may be one and a half times the allotted deadline for their non-disabled peers. The point being that they are expected to learn the same content at the same pace and rigor with accommodations to how they are taught, or how they are required to respond. Conversely, modification of a student's work means the work they are required to do is changed, or modified, from that required of their non-disabled peers. Modifications change content such that the students are no longer expected to learn at the same pace or rigor. In short, accommodations change *how* a student is taught, modifications change *what* a student is taught. An example of a student with modifications may have severe cognitive deficits that require them to continue to practice a basic math skill, like counting to 10, when their non-disabled peers are learning division. A summary comparison of 504 Plan and IEP defining characteristics is provided in Table 1.

Table 1
Summary Comparison Table for 504 Plans and IEP

	504 Plan	IEP
Law	Civil Rights protection under Americans with Disabilities Act	Education law enacted by Individuals with Disabilities Education Act (IDEA)
Eligibility Determinants	Disability significantly impairs a major life function, with or without an educational impact.	Disability meets criteria of one of the IDEA 13 qualifying categories, significantly impacts educational performance, and requires specialized services.
Possible Plan Supports	Academic accommodations, some modifications, and related services.	Academic accommodations, modifications, specialized courses, and related services.
Committee Decisions	Plan determinations are made by a committee of qualified persons (usually school personnel) with knowledge of the student. Parents are invited for input.	Plan determinations are made by a committee including: parent, designee, data interpreter, general education teacher, and special education teacher. Must have at least three people to represent the five committee roles.
Reviews and Renewals	Annual reviews are held to determine current needs. Redetermination of services is required every three years.	Annual reviews are held to determine current needs. Redetermination of services is required every three years.

Accommodations and modifications are meant to ensure differentiated instruction for students with 504 Plans and IEPs. That said, a fervent passion of all educators should be to give every student the opportunity to reach their maximum potential. That passion makes it imperative to have high expectations for each student, whether they have a 504 Plan, IEP, or no identified disability. A child will only rise to the level of expectation we set for them. It is important to teach all our students to become self-evident and independent. It is critical, therefore, to teach them to cope within their environment instead of manipulating the environment to help them cope.

Educational Settings (Placement)

The goal of having alternate educational settings is to provide the support and structure needed for each child to find academic and social-emotional success on their way to becoming productive members of society. With that being said, the best setting for any child is in the general education setting with their non-disabled peers. It is also the goal of any support structure to provide a path to join or rejoin a general education classroom. For a long time, students who did not learn at the pace of others or had behavior difficulties that interrupted their learning, or that of others, were removed from class or from school all together through suspension or alternate educational settings. With the amount of research showing that exclusionary practices are more detrimental to educational outcomes and with the wonderful trend towards inclusionary instruction there are new challenges around how to best manage the behaviors seen in our classrooms. I want to take a moment to briefly describe each of the typical placement settings used in education, by order of least restrictive environment (LRE), before I discuss the important topic of behavior planning. The education settings I will introduce are summarized in Table 2.

Table 2
Educational Placement and Settings

Settings	Description	Location
General Education	The least restrictive environment: student is taught with non-disabled peers.	Regular classroom with one teacher and the state mandated number of students, or less.
Co-Teaching or Inclusion	Student is taught with non-disabled peers with the added support of a second teacher or paraprofessional.	Regular classroom with a second adult to help teach (licensed teacher) or support students (paraprofessional).
Resource Classroom	Student leaves the general education setting for small group instruction by a special education teacher.	Special Education classroom with a teacher to student ratio of 1:8 if there is a paraprofessional in the classroom, also, there can be up to 10 students.
Self-Contained Classroom	Students receive all, or most, of their education in this single setting.	Special Education classroom with ratios of 1:6, 1:10, or 1:15, depending on student needs
Alternate Learning Environment (ALE)	Students may receive all or part of their education in this single setting.	This is not a special education designated classroom but may have up to 1/3 of the students with an IEP.
Therapeutic Day Treatment (TDT)	Students attend a mental health facility during the day to receive education and therapy services.	This is not a special education designated program but students may be placed in TDT via an IEP.
Residential	Students attend a mental health facility as an in patient until discharged by the treatment team.	This is not a special education designated program but students may be placed in a residential program via an IEP.

General Education Setting

The general education setting is the regular classroom with a teacher and state specified number of students (determined by grade level) where learning takes place at the scope, sequence, pace, and rigor of the mandated content curriculum. This setting is the least restrictive environment, meaning the students are learning in a setting that is most like their non-disabled peers. The general education setting is the typical classroom for most students to learn academically and social-emotionally. In this setting, classroom differentiated instruction, or classroom accommodations, should be a common practice to meet the needs of all learners. In this setting, some students may need additional differentiation or accommodations specific to their disability as would be addressed in their 504 Plan or IEP. However, instruction occurs alongside their non-disabled peers with accommodations implemented as needed.

Co-Teaching or Inclusion Setting

Under this model of teaching the students are still learning in the general education classroom but there is a second teacher in the class to help teach, support students, and offer opportunities for Tier 2 academic supports, as may be seen in small group instruction strategies. In some districts, a paraprofessional may provide push-in services for inclusion support when a second teacher is not available. The IEP or 504 Plan should specify the support(s) and educational setting(s) that have been identified for the student.

Resource Setting

A resource setting is a separate classroom for small group instruction. In this setting the teacher to student ratio is maximized at one to eight, unless there is a paraprofessional in the classroom, then the ratio can be two (teacher and paraprofessional) to ten; but cannot exceed that student number without a waiver from the State Education Agency (SEA). Resource classrooms are generally specific to reading, writing, and math, but in higher grades (secondary) some districts may offer resource courses in Science and Social Studies. Though it is very appropriate with the amount of math, writing, and reading in these two subjects they are not areas assessed for qualification so are often overlooked when placing students in academic settings or master planning for campuses.

Self-Contained Setting

The self-contained classroom has different configurations. The most common configurations are for the students who are identified to have severe cognitive impairment or are catastrophically disabled. Depending on student needs, the class sizes are limited to ensure the faculty and staff can meet their individual needs. Most of these classrooms are designated as 1:6, 1:10, or 1:15 for the teach to student ratio, where the lower ratio is reserved for the students with the highest needs. A designated behavior self-contained classroom will often have the same general requirements as a resource classroom, but requirements can vary by state and by school district. Please discuss self-contained setting requirements with your SEA based on your school district's specific circumstances and needs.

Alternate Learning Environment (ALE) Setting

An alternate learning environment (ALE) can be represented in several ways. Many districts have specific guidelines for ALE classrooms that should be explored in your own state before creating one on your campus. They are generally limited to around 18 students and can have students identified with a disability through a 504 Plan, and IEP, or students without an identified disability. However, there are often state-mandated restrictions for placing students in an ALE setting so please review your state's requirements.

Therapeutic Day Treatment (TDT) Setting

A Therapeutic Day Treatment (TDT) setting is provided by a mental health service agency. The students attend school at the facility and receive therapy during the day. These students go home to their families at the end of the school day. Placement in these settings can be school mandated or by voluntary parental/guardian admission. Insurance can help offset some of the expenses associated with TDT, and there are many factors that influence cost. I recommend referring parents and families considering TDT settings to consult with social case workers in their region for assistance in navigating these services.

Residential Setting

A residential placement setting generally begins with an acute admission during a mental health crisis (student shows a likely or expressed imminent harm to themselves or others) that can last anywhere from three days to two weeks and students are admitted to the mental hospital facility. This initial admittance can be extended to a residential placement until the student is deemed safe to themselves and others, when they are medically cleared for discharge.

Behavior Intervention Plan (BIP)

A behavior Intervention Plan (BIP) is a document that includes the description of the behavior, or behaviors being addressed, probable triggers or reasons for the exhibited behavior, and the interventions, strategies, and services that will be used to best support the student's needs. Generally, the behavioral support will be based on positive intervention strategies and be specific to address the behavior's frequency, duration, and intensity when determining how progress will be measured and when to redirect the efforts of the plan. Though a BIP is most frequently seen in terms of meeting the needs of a student served under a 504 Plan or an IEP, a behavior support plan can be used for any student in need, regardless of disability or identification. The BIP is a requirement when the student is being served for a mental illness disability and should be a part of the intervention process for students with a Chronic or Mental Illness behavior type as described in Chapter two. Short term behavior incentive plans are good interventions for students affected by Episodic Behavior and help prevent them from becoming Chronic Behavior. Having an understanding of behavior and intervention strategies can make classroom management in a general education setting easier to obtain and fosters a more effective learning environment for all.

Behavior plans are written for students who have been identified with behaviors that are pervasive and impede the student's ability to learn or interferes with the ability of others to learn in a shared educational setting. They are most appropriate when the student is not responding to general classroom management interventions or school-wide positive behavior supports. Behavior plans may also be written for students whose behavior may pose a physical risk to themselves or others before removing them to a more restrictive environment. However, it is important to note that a student being removed from the general education setting to a more restrictive environment because of behavior should have a BIP to support a path to return to the general education setting. This process is suitable for students removed from school and/or students subject to disciplinary actions that may have been determined a result of their disability. Caution is warranted with this statement as a student cannot be disciplined for their disability. However, a student may have a behavior that exhibits as impulsivity but understands right from wrong. This particular student may still be subject to school discipline policies based on the behavior action and disability of the student. The special education committee will determine whether the behavior is a manifestation of the disability and next steps to help the student make a different choice in the future; steps that must be documented in the BIP.

Content of a Behavior Intervention Plan

The BIP must describe the baseline measure of the targeted behaviors to include the frequency, duration, and intensity. These measures should come from a variety of data sources and collected across different settings, times of day, and activities to create an opportunity to identify trends in behaviors. After the data have been collected and analyzed, goals and objectives for new target behavior will be written along with interventions designed to support those behavior changes. These criteria will be very important in helping determine whether the interventions are working and whether any adjustments need to be made to make them more effective over time.

Much of the behavior data collected will identify the antecedent event, the behavior exhibited by the student, and the consequence issued; the ABCs of behavior monitoring. The BIP should include strategies that may offer alternatives to the triggering event and help prevent the behavior from happening. Communication is often the trigger and an area where teachers can be coached to more successfully support their students. A slight perspective change from a negative to a positive focus in communication makes a huge difference for students with challenging behavior. An example may be something as simple as the wording used to redirect a student. Instead of telling a student to sit down or receive a clip down (on a clip or down system), remind them that if they are in their seat they may get to earn a clip up. At the same time there is student accountability in the BIP. The plan should help teach adaptive behaviors to the student that will foster self-efficacy and independence while promoting self-awareness, self-regulation, and improved interpersonal skills. These lessons can be reinforced through consequences, both positive and negative, used to influence the student's behavior choices. Finally, the plan should incorporate a measure of the efficacy for the interventions that follow the S.M.A.R.T. goal format so they are Specific, Measurable, Attainable, Realistic, and Time-bound. Another word of caution is that having a BIP does not mean the behaviors suddenly disappear. In fact, it takes a good measure of time to change behavior. I do not personally agree with the adage of changing behavior. From my perspective, we work to replace undesirable behavior with desirable behavior.

Cognitive Behavior Intervention

Cognitive Behavior Intervention (CBI) is the integration of thoughts, feelings, and behaviors into the training and support of new thinking models for the students and the adults who work with them. In my research I identified what I call a *Paradigm Fulcrum* that is the point where individuals move from thoughts to action (Davis, 2019a, 2019b). What I learned in my research is that we can only determine a change in an individual, group, or organization through evidence of a cognitive change, a paradigm change, or a behavior change. Cognitive

change can come in two forms: how we feel about something and how we think about something. If someone says or does something that hurts our feelings, we tend to *think* negatively based on our feelings. Or, if we have a great experience that makes us feel good, we tend to have positive thoughts. The cognitive changes we have, good or bad, shape the framework through which we interpret the experience, our *paradigm*. As an example, we have a student in school who begins the school year by regularly disrupting the classroom with negative behaviors. The teacher may *feel* somewhat offended by the recurring behavior causing the teacher to form an opinion about the child (*think* a certain way) and then create a paradigm that frames their interpretation of the student's actions. Simply stated, the teacher's expectations for the student is created from within their paradigm of the child. The teacher may say the student is a problem child or is a bad kid. Within this paradigm, the behavior of the teacher towards the student is now predisposed for a negative interaction. However, let's say that this same teacher has learned that this student lost a grandparent over the summer. It would be a fairly safe assumption that the teacher's additional thoughts would foster an emotional reaction (empathy) towards the Episodic Behavior the student is exhibiting. That feeling of empathy about the scenario would change how the teacher thought about the student's behavior, which would change their paradigm for interpreting their interactions and effect the behavior produced by both parties. Changing how we interact and initiating the *Paradigm Fulcrum* towards a positive interpersonal experience is a major contributor to student achievement as evidenced by John Hattie's research on effect size and influences on learning (Hattie, 2017).

In most cognitive behavior models thinking is initiated before thinking, but it is my opinion that feelings are the influencers for our thinking. In my consideration, our feelings come from an innate emotional response to some outside stimulus that trigger a basic emotion for happiness, sadness, fear, or anger or any range of those emotions that we feel automatically. The reaction to our feelings occur in the rational, thinking, part of our brain, though it may be too quick to identify as it shifts from our emotional brain to our rational brain. The rational part of our brain tells our body how to react physically.

Epstein (1991) was the first to describe the modern two-brain theory of personality in his work on cognitive-experiential self-theory (CEST). In his two-brain concept, Epstein explained that our emotional brains are hard-wired for destructive thought processes. This hard wiring served a useful survival purpose for protecting early humans from apex predators, but today can cause behavioral and psychological challenges when not understood and operationalized in a constructive way. For example, as we live our life our emotional brain is constantly assessing our experiences and the environment for threats to our psychological well-being and physical survival. Perceived threats are met with very quick fight, flight, or freeze responses. Social-emotional intelligence is important to learn and teach as the learned ability to interrupt this automatic process using constructive thinking and action goal setting (i.e, purposeful problem solving) (Epstein, 1991; Nelson et al., 2017).

The concepts of social-emotional learning for students and transformative emotional intelligence skills for adults are rooted in the notion that the uniquely human competencies of self-awareness, self-regulation, social awareness, and relational regulation require soft skills found in the interpersonal, intrapersonal, self-management, and personal leadership dimensions of transformative emotional intelligence (TEI). I will talk more about TEI in chapter five. The important concept to take from this section is the idea that people can positively influence and replace their behavior over time and through purposeful practice. Learned behaviors that have been interpreted as enhancing to one's psychological well-being or physical survival because injury or death were avoided may be either negative or positive from the societal context. When behaviors are negative, learning new responses to experiences so the brain can learn to automatically choose a more productive reaction is the goal of the cognitive behavior interventions that must be included BIPs. The structure needed to learn these new habits and ways of forming constructive thinking should be planned in education using a multi-tiered system of support.

Multi-Tiered Systems of Support (MTSS)

A multi-tiered system of support uses an evidence-based framework to provide whole-child education and intervention integrating academic achievement, SEL, and mental health and behavior needs for students. The National Association of School Psychologists created a crosswalk planning worksheet to help districts coordinate their practices under eight categories of *Essential Schools Practices*:

1. Effective, coordinated use of data that informs instruction, student and school outcomes, and school accountability.
2. Comprehensive, rigorous curricula provided to *ALL* students.
3. Effective coordination of services across systems and within schools.
4. Use of evidence-based comprehensive learning supports.
5. Integration of comprehensive school mental and behavioral health services into learning supports.
6. Integration of school climate and safety efforts into school improvement efforts.
7. Provision of high quality, relevant professional development.
8. Maintain a comprehensive accountability system.

It is the premise of the MTSS that I propose the Davis Performance Model as a framework to support mental health and behavior in schools.

Davis Performance Model

To integrate this important discussion on behavior, I have created a model to provide a structure for behavior support in schools. The Davis Performance Model should be used as a framework guide for planning and providing proactive support structures, professional development opportunities for faculty and staff, student success plans, goal setting for IEP and 504 meetings, school safety planning, school-based mental health planning, campus master planning, and discipline policy planning. The alternative seems to be to rely on reactive and punitive actions that have proven to be mostly ineffective and have likely contributed to the behavior crises we are seeing in 21st century schools. This model provides the foundation for teacher preparation and development from my administrator understanding and perspective that the traditional *one-size-fits-all* education model does not and cannot work for many children. In fact, *one-size-fits-all* education seems to be the genesis of all things that need education reform. We need reform in mental health and behavior understanding, support, and interventions that are system wide and include the integration of school-wide positive behavior interventions, supports, and restorative discipline (Vincent et al., 2016)The Davis Performance Model provides a structure to begin framing conversations so that planning can become more appropriate for each school to support the individual community populations they serve.

Situational Behavior

For this discussion, I define situational behavior as caused by internal or external factors that can affect the emotional response system and is usually temporary in nature.

> Information about the current situation is crucial to action control. In the simplest scenario, responses are triggered and controlled by "stimuli" present in the situation. Besides external stimuli, the sources of which are in the environment outside the organism, internal stimuli arise within the organism itself. These internal stimuli may be transient states of the organism such as hunger or states such as internal conflict. (Beckmann & Heckhausen, 2018, p. 114)

Some examples of internal situational behavior factors may be that an individual is hungry (EthosHealth, 2017; Shabat-Simon et al., 2018), or perhaps tired (Coulombe et al., 2011; McCarthy, 2017; Merk Manuals, 2020; Wheaton et al., 2016). Some examples of external situational behavior factors may be frustration or irritability that can be triggered by game or peer play, perceived threats, or activities that feel difficult to the youth (Leibenluft, 2017).

Episodic Behavior

In this discussion I define episodic behavior to be a result of a life event such as a divorce, death, birth of a sibling, move, or other high duress situation. "At times, the reasons behind some of the behaviors your children exhibit may not always be obvious, and there may be a situational factor that is influencing their reaction" ("Situational Factors," 2020, par. 1). There are social and biological factors that play a part in how an individual experiences an event, how they respond to that event, and their coping resiliency. Over time, situational or episodic factors have the potential to increase the risk of developing disruptive behavior disorders (Liu et al., 2017; National Council for Behavioral Health, 2016; Wertz et al., 2016).

Chronic Behavior

  Chronic behavior is a result of unresolved situational behavior or episodic behavior that has become habitual and interferes with expected milestones or outcomes in learning academically and social-emotionally. I consider these to be a mental health challenge, but not necessarily a mental health disorder. "A mental health challenge is a broader term including both mental disorders and symptoms of mental disorders that may not be severe enough to warrant the diagnosis of a mental disorder" (National Council for Behavioral Health, 2016, p. 4). The Main Place (2020) extends that definition as "any disease or condition affecting the brain that influences the way a person thinks, feels, behaves, and/or relates to others and to their surroundings…Many mental health challenges are caused by a combination of genetic, biological, psychological, and environmental factors" (*Mental Health Challenges*, n.d.). It is important to understand that chronic behavior can be a result of a mental health disorder, but this conversation is only to glean an understanding and develop empathy in the planning and training that must be done.

This discussion is not a diagnostic tool or diagnostic framework.

Mental Illness or Disorder

In my Davis Performance Model, I describe mental illness as something identified and diagnosed by a licensed health provider. I also indicate that this behavior type requires the most planning to best serve and support their needs in the educational setting. The American Psychiatric Association defined mental illnesses as "health conditions involving changes in emotion, thinking or behavior (or a combination of these). Mental illnesses are associated with distress and/or problems functioning in social, work or family activities" (*What Is Mental Illness?*, 2018).

Key Takeaways of the Davis Performance Model

When using this framework model it is important to recognize two key takeaways for its purpose:

1. This book and the Davis Performance Model is **_not_** a diagnostic tool. Only a licensed professional can, or should, make a diagnosis.

2. This book and the Davis Performance Model *is* a conversation framework for planning.

The next two pages summarize the four Behavior Types, the four Behavior Intervention Tiers, and the parameters and settings that should be considered when master planning for supports and staffing, safety and crisis planning, and success planning in schools. Again, this is not a program, rather a framework document for strategic planning, training, and support for the schools, families, and students to better partner and learn to manage the mental health and behavior needs of students. As previously noted, one in five students will fall within the Episodic and/or Chronic Types of Behavior, and one in ten students will be in the Mental Illness Behavior Type. If your district is not proactively supporting and training teachers, administrators, paraprofessionals, all of the support staff, and their students and the existing protocols are reactive towards these issues, then we need to talk.

Behavior Types	Behavior Frequency	Behavior Duration	Behavior Intensity	Behavior Intervention Tier	Educational Setting
Situational Behavior: child may be tired, hungry, or just 'in a bad mood'. This does not constitute a possible mental health issue.	Infrequent (less than 2 times per week) or sporadic; occasional occurrences	Short term a few minutes to a few hours; less than or up to a single day	Mild to tantrum, but due to frequency and duration still considered a mild behavior dysregulation	Tier 1 Intervention: can be predominantly managed through classroom practices and procedures by the teach with occasional support from another adult.	General education classroom, possible support from the administrative office (principal's office), or a team teacher.
Episodic Behavior: child is experiencing behavioral changes due to a life event such as divorce, death, or other high duress situation. May also be caused by Situational Behavior that becomes habitual. This may become a possible mental health issue.	Frequent (2-3 times per week) or recurs over a prolonged period of time (number of consecutive days)	Short term for length of time the behavior is exhibited to long term (up to six months)	Mild to tantrum, frequency and duration are more prevalent and can happen 2-3 times per week and persist up to six months	Tier 1 and Tier 2 Intervention: much of the Episodic Behavior should try to be managed at the Tier 1 level. However, the student may need Tier 2 support by using pull-out or push-in support from the school counselor or a therapist to help mitigate the behaviors.	General education classroom, counselor's office, therapy room

Behavior Types	Behavior Frequency	Behavior Duration	Behavior Intensity	Behavior Intervention Tier	Educational Setting
Chronic Behavior: child has unresolved Situational Behavior or Episodic Behavior that has become habitual and is interfering with expected milestones or outcomes in learning academically and social-emotionally. This is a mental health issue but may not be a mental illness.	Frequent (2-3 times per week) and prolonged over time.	Behavior is pervasive in the student's day and across settings.	Intensity can range from refusal to complete tasks to destruction of property and attempts to harm self or others.	Depending on the behavior intensity, Tier 1 and Tier 2 interventions should be implemented when possible. Tier 3 interventions will likely include a behavior support plan, regular therapy appointments and possible medical consultation for pharmaceutical interventions.	General education classroom, special education classroom, counselor's office, principal's office, therapy room, possible outside school therapy or medical support
Mental Illness: child has developed a mental illness or has a mental illness that is being identified by a mental health professional. This behavior type requires the most planning how to best serve students with emotional dysregulation.	Frequent (2-3 times per week) and prolonged over time.	Behavior is pervasive in the student's day and across settings.	Intensity can range from refusal to complete tasks to destruction of property and attempts to harm self or others.	Like Chronic Behavior, Tiers 1, 2, and 3 interventions should all be used to support these students. Additionally, Tier 4 interventions may need to be implemented. Tier 4 support may add changes in the educational setting,	General education classroom, special education classroom, counselor's office, principal's office, therapy room, possible outside school therapy or medical support, therapeutic day treatment (TDT), or residential treatment (mental hospital setting)

Chapter 4: Teacher Support and Training on Mental Health and Behavior

Educator Attrition and Burnout

Nationwide it is reported that we have an 8% attrition rate among new teachers. There is a large body of research on the topic of teacher attrition and burnout (Gonzalez-Roma et al., 2006; Maslach et al., 2001; Perrone et al., 2019; Rumschlag, 2017; Shackleton et al., 2019; Skaalvik & Skaalvik, 2017). A walk down the halls of many schools will reveal a level of teacher frustration and its adverse effects on morale, teaching practices, and student achievement. Adding to the pressures already experienced by school personnel, the mental health and behavior crisis welling up in our schools is showing up in the literature on schools and district practices worldwide. Researchers from around the globe are beginning to report similar statistics on the occurrence of behavioral challenges related to mental health in the primary and secondary school settings (Bolier et al., 2013; Child Mind Institute, 2016; Curby et al., 2015; Ford et al., 2017; Haidt & Paresky, 2019; Merikangas et al., 2009; O'Connor & Cameron, 2017).

This book is an attempt to unite our conversations into a global dialogue about what the phenomena are, how can we structure a proactive support system and reform the practices that simply do not work and extend the practices that do. A large part of the solution lies in educator preparation and development programs that can better equip us to identify, manage, and teach constructive thinking and purposeful behaviors. The next part of this discussion brings several initiatives to lights that could be considered under whole-school planning conversations.

Educator Preparation, Development, and Support

I have always found it interesting that we agree to not place a teacher into a classroom without training them, making them prove proficiency, and obtaining a license in their content area before we allow them to begin a teaching or administrative career. Along this thought, we would not allow a math teacher to instruct an English class without the same process in place. Yet, we ask teachers with no training, knowledge, or proficiency to teach social-emotional learning skills to students alongside their academic content. There are many SEL programs available on the market and my intention is not to endorse one over another. In fact, the Rand Corporation has identified 60 SEL intervention programs that meet ESSA guidelines for campus plans that may increase potential funding for the district under Title 1, Title 2, and Title 4 as a Tier four intervention (S. Grant et al., 2017; Sean Grant et al., 2017). What I am advocating is a change in teacher and administrator preparation and development programs to include in the curriculum components of transformative emotional intelligence, Mental Health First Aid, School-Based Mental Health, and Behavior Management Training for parents and school personnel. Such a curriculum would focus on coaching teachers with the thought processes and skills to interact more effectively with students and respond proactively to their behavior needs, regardless of the behavior type they are trying to manage. Another benefit of experiencing such a curriculum would be a reduction in the adverse effects of teacher and support staff burnout, including attrition from the profession.

Teacher Support

Teacher support comes in many forms: preparation for licensing programs, professional development training, in-school support by colleagues and administrators, support from the families and caregivers, community support, and self-care, all of which are equally important to the success and longevity of a teacher's career. In this chapter, I will spend a little time making suggestions for talking points for your district under these support areas. Using them to help guide your discussions can open more areas or expand those that would be applicable to your specific campus or district needs.

Licensing Preparation and Professional Development

Educator preparation programs, whether for teacher, administrator, or program director, should include two types of training that are not currently required or offered. The first type of training is the development of the education professional's emotional intelligence skills. Many times when I am asked to observe a class to offer suggestions for behavior management, I find the student is exhibiting behaviors which are being escalated by the adult. In a recent situation I found an educational professional who deals with anxiety and PTSD attempting to work with a child with oppositional, explosive, and physical behavior that triggered the adult's own dysregulated behavior. The result was a toxic and unproductive environment that was a detriment to both the child and the adult. Fortunately, I have had the opportunity to coach the adult and she is becoming more of an asset and ally for the students now that she is paying attention to her own feelings and working to develop her own emotional skills. I predict that these experiences will engender healing on some levels for both the student and adult. That healing, in turn, will enable trust and facilitate the academic progress of the student.

The second type of training that needs to happen is basic behavior management that covers all four types of behavior as outlined in chapter two. I remember being told when I first completed my teacher preparation program that I would come to my first day of school with my notebook all together with my lesson plans and ready to teach my eager students and would want to toss it by the end of first period when I realized what *real* students were like in the classroom. We spend time making teachers understand content and lesson planning but do nothing to help them plan or understand the student behaviors they experience or what to do when things go wrong in the classroom. We never hear a teacher say they are leaving their district, the classroom or the educational industry because they did not like their content. They leave because they become disenchanted with *teaching*. To overcome this problem and achieve true education reform, educator preparation programs, educator professional development programs, mentoring programs, and district or campus policy programs must support the development of teacher knowledge and skills related to behavior management to help them develop their own personal skill sets to be best equipped to enter and stay in education.

> Sometimes removing a student, or excessively deferring to someone else, can minimize the authority of the teacher. Find the

Classroom Management Support

Classroom management support comes from different sources. The first line of support is from self-care. Educators who self-care, develop their emotional skills, and practice self-awareness are much better at supporting the needs of their students. Educators who do not self-care and develop themselves emotionally are the ones who find teaching to be overwhelming and succumb to stress and burnout.

> Self-care is not a waste of time. Self-care makes your use of time more sustainable.
>
> -Jackie Viramontez

Classroom management support can also come from colleagues or peers. Appropriate conversations about classroom management to draw on the experience or ideas of others is a great way to develop skills. Appropriateness is related to the maintenance of confidentiality, as well as not allowing the conversation to turn negative. Maintaining positive encounters builds trust and resilience by leaving participants feeling hopeful and re-energized about the future.

Administrators can also be a source of classroom support. Whether they are coming into a classroom to help redirect a student's behavior, pulling the student from the classroom (i.e. – student goes to the principal's office), utilizing Tier two tag-team supports, can increase the efficacy of everyone involved, and it can change the outcome for that student's day.

District and Campus Discipline Policy Support

One interesting phenomenon I have noted during my years of experience in education is lack of conversations that happen across districts that could deepen the effectiveness of discipline policies and increase continuity between grades within buildings, and even campuses within districts. I want to restate that having a *one-size-fits-all* approach is not appropriate nor my intention. Rather, a commonality across classes and campuses that includes an appropriate high level of expectation for each student increases the likelihood that all students will meet standards because this level of alignment helps ensure that each student has the right supports in place to be successful. In the next chapter I will delve deeper into the types of continuity and supports that can provide discussion frameworks for developing some solution strategies to address mental health and behavior challenges in schools.

Chapter 5: Integrating Supports for Addressing Mental Health Issues and Problematic student Behaviors

There are positive and common sentiments around the ideal of teaching the whole child. I am going to take a moment to revisit some fundamental theories that support the integration of feelings, thinking, and learning that helped lay the foundation to the whole-child concept. I feel this review is necessary to help educators understand that there is not a separation in the roles of educating our children. Many times I hear that school is for content learning and everything else should be taught at home by the parents. As educators we see the child for most of the waking part of the day. Parents see the students for a short period of time in the morning before school and a few hours after school before bedtime. I am going to step up to my podium for a moment and make myself vulnerable by just restating the adage that it takes a village to raise a child; we must all own the education and development of every child. Every student is learning from us in everything we do. We constantly model how to be in this world. It *is* our responsibility to teach them everything we can, content or not, by integrating social-emotional learning into our content and leading by example in modeling our own TEI skills in every interaction. Let me lay the foundation for this argument.

Cognitive Behavior Theory

Cognitive Behavior Theory has flourished with interventions for children and adolescents under the assumptions that "(1) cognitive activity affects behavior, (2) cognitive activity may be monitored and altered, and (3) behavior change may be achieved through cognitive change" (Hupp et al., 2008, p. 263). The Handbook of Clinical Psychology defined *cognitive* as a reference to covert behavior, which are thoughts and mental images not readily seen by others to differentiate it from the overt behavior, referring to the actions seen by others. When setting interventions for students it is important to plan in terms of cognitive behavior training which would include how they feel, think, and act.

Positive Behavior Interventions and Supports (PBIS)

Positive behavior supports are important to engage student motivation to change and promoting the desired behavior. There is a commercial program called Positive Behavior Interventions and Supports (PBIS) (*PBIS.org*, 2019) that many schools incorporate alongside Response to Intervention (RtI) as a two-pronged, whole-school initiative. The Office of Special Education Programs and Office of Elementary and Secondary Education began a

Technical Assistance Center on PBIS to improve the capacity of SEAs, LEAs, and schools to establish, scale-up, and sustain the PBIS framework to (a) scale up tier 2 and 3 systems to improve outcomes for students with or at-risk for disabilities, (b) enhance school climate and school safety, and (c) improve conditions for learning to promote the well-being of all students (*PBIS.org*, 2019)

Whole School, Whole Community, Whole Child Model

Coordinated school health began by understanding the positive outcomes of supporting student learning and academic achievement along with positive mental health and behavior interventions and strategies. But these efforts were stronger when partnered with family and community members. Through extensive planning and research, evidence emerged to suggest "that education and health are reciprocally interactive – that healthier students simply learn better; and that more educated adults live healthier, wealthier, and longer" (Kolbe et al., 2015). From this research came a model called the *Whole School, Whole Community, Whole Child* (WSCC) model as a collaborative approach to learning and health.

Integrated Learning

It has become apparent that supporting mental health and behaviors alongside academic training in schools is a natural evolution of the educational model. Recent legislative changes through the Every Student Succeeds Act (ESSA) "provides significant opportunity to increase access to comprehensive school psychology services to help improve student and school outcomes" (*ESSA Mental and Behavioral Health Services for School Psychologists*, 2019, par. 1). What is most encouraging is the increased funding opportunities that may be available to meet the mental health and behavior needs of students. In an open acknowledgement of the direct link between the mental health and behavioral wellness of students and their academic achievement, ESSA also outlines the understanding of the impact on school climate, high school graduation rates, risky behaviors, and discipline rates. Authorization for funding opportunities under Title I, Title II, and Title IV opens many possibilities for districts; especially those identified as in need of targeted support and improvement (*ESSA Mental and Behavioral Health Services for School Psychologists*, 2019; Sean Grant et al., 2017). Some of the efforts supported by ESSA include:

- Implement multitiered systems of support (MTSS), positive behavior interventions and support, or other school-wide tiered models to address the social–emotional, behavioral, and mental health needs of all students.

- Administer universal mental and behavioral screening and provide early intervention for at-risk students.

- Increase access to comprehensive school mental and behavioral health services, including wellness promotion.

- Improve quality and effectiveness of family engagement and school community mental health partnerships.
- Provide mental health first aid and other professional development and training for relevant school staff to:
  - Facilitate early identification and referral of students who may be in need of mental health supports.
  - Implement suicide prevention policies and practices, including suicide risk and threat assessment.
  - Support the implementation of trauma informed practices.
  - Increase knowledge of culturally competent practices.
  - Support evidence-based efforts to prevent school violence, bullying, and harassment; improve school safety; and foster safe and supportive learning environments.

School Based Mental Health Programs (SBMH)

School-Based Mental Health Programs (SBMH) are identification and intervention programs that implement a network of mental health and behavioral services within the school site. The best practice principles of a SBMH program would include:

- Early identification of mental health or behavior needs in students.
- Coordinated efforts between home, school, and the community resources.
- Service integration maintains the student and their family as the focus for intervention or service decisions.
- Services and interventions offered should be culturally sensitive and competent
- The ultimate goals of SBMH should be inclusive education with considerations for attendance and academic success.
- All interventions and supports should be research based, data driven, and results oriented.
- Should consider technology as a supplement to services as may be seen with telecommunications or teletherapy.

Mental Health First Aid (MHFA)

Mental Health First Aid (MHFA) is a national program that offers a skills-based training course that teaches participants about mental health and substance-use issues (*Mental Health First Aid USA*, 2020). Participants learn important skills in this training program to include:

- Growing their knowledge of signs, symptoms, and risk factors of mental illnesses and addictions.

- Identifying multiple types of professional and self-help resources for individuals with a mental illness or addiction.

- Increasing their confidence in and likelihood to help an individual in distress.

- Showing increased mental wellness themselves.

There are currently Mental Health First Aid trainings available for *Youth*, which is for adults working with youth; *Adult*, which is for adults working with adults; and *Teen*, which is for teens learning to identify peers in need of support. The premise of this training is to help build awareness of mental health challenges and disorders as well as substance use. The individuals trained in MHFA are not qualified to diagnose or give advice, rather 'notice' when someone may need support and make sure they are connected to the right resources.

Behavior Management Training

Just as educators are prepared to develop and present lessons, they need to be prepared to effectively interact with students, colleagues, families, and their communities. A component of Behavior Management Training (BMT) is the development of emotional intelligence skills, another piece is learning how to interact with others who may be experiencing a mental health issue or disorder or exhibiting a behavioral outburst that would benefit from effective intervention strategies. There are several certification programs available and most education regional service centers offer behavior management training that exceeds basic classroom management techniques. I encourage districts to explore training for their faculty and staff along with parents and caregivers.

Chapter 5 Summary

This chapter lays the foundation for the argument that teaching and learning are holistically connected through the emotional mind, the rational mind, and experiences in a complex and integrated process. Current research trends, knowledge on learning, mental health and behavior and legislative changes continue to evolve into a multi-tiered system of supports that consider and develop the whole child. Understanding the need to integrate learning, knowing how to do it, and being trained to do it are different facets of the success plan that must be developed. This chapter provides just some of the framework for conversations that are research-based, data driven, and results oriented.

Chapter 6: Solutions for Schools Supporting Mental Health and Behavior

Educational Reform to Support Mental Health and Behavior in Schools

Supporting mental health needs and replacing negative behavior in schools is a top priority. I purposely left the word *students* out of that opening statement. Recognizing that the adults in education are grown up versions of the students they serve, the statistics we currently see in the schools should be an indication of the need for the interventions I am suggesting we provide for all stakeholders. Adults need their own emotional intelligence developed to be the best versions of themselves so they can, in turn, better serve the students in their classrooms. Administrators need the same skills development opportunities to help them be better campus and educational leaders. What many districts overlook, is the need for paraprofessional support and training, as well.

Reform Teacher Support and Training

I have mentioned several times in this book that teachers need training to develop their own skills before they can help develop those of their students. I took this belief to the teachers and started a research project with Gary Low, Professor Emeritus, Texas A&M University – Kingsville; Richard Hammett, Walden University; and David Christian, University of Arkansas. It was my belief that teachers did not take on new responsibilities over four objections. First, the teachers do not understand the initiative or expectation. This goes back to the issue that they are predominantly prepared to know their content and how to write a lesson plan before entering the classroom but may not have the tools in their box to layer curriculum requirements outside their training. Second, even if they do have an understanding of the initiative or expectation, they do not know how to implement it into their daily activities, or what to do if it does not work with the students. No one wants to be a failure at their job. Many will avoid the work before being, or feeling, unsuccessful at the task. Teachers are really no different in this regard than the students who they ask to complete assignments on topics that may not be well understood. Third, teachers avoid tasks because they already feel overwhelmed and that one more thing on their plate is too much. Given the scope, sequence, pace, and rigor of their content, when would they have time to implement another set of lessons or curriculum? So, they don't do it. Finally, they do not see any value in the added responsibilities; they feel there is no monetary benefit that can be realized. Using this information our research project was created to test these obstacles and attempt to overcome them. Below is the study description and initial observations from the project. At the time of this writing the study is not quite complete, and the data have not yet been fully analyzed. The discussion below, therefore, is based on anecdotal observations.

The Teacher Development Book Study: SEL/TEI for K-12 Educators

Emotional Intelligence is not something that is just developed as a skillset in adulthood. In fact, to be more productive, successful, and happy as an adult it is important to work to develop these skills over your lifetime. Within the school system, teaching Emotional Intelligence to children is called Socio-Emotional Learning, or Social-Emotional Learning, (SEL) and should be taught and practiced throughout the educational trek. It is my belief that teachers resist new educational initiatives or fail to implement with fidelity because of three reasons: (1) they do not understand it, (2) they do not know how to use it, or (3) they feel it is just one more thing on their plate. The support needs of our youth are changing and the rise of social-emotional dysfunction in our schools is driving teachers from the profession, and students into home-schooling. As a result, I believe the need to implement emotional intelligence into our daily practices is more important than ever. The reason for embedding emotional intelligence is partly to improve the educational experience for everyone, and partly because it is the missing piece needed to help develop our children into responsible, capable, self-evident adults who are ready to function within society and global communities. It was for these reasons that I created an exploratory case study project to help teachers understand Emotional Intelligence, learn to develop their own skills, practice embedded skills into their lesson plans as SEL learning standards, and collect and analyze data for accountability and instructional design. The exploratory case study covered most of the school year with free, embedded professional development and a time commitment from participants of about 90 minutes per week. The major study objectives were broken into the following four parts.

    The first part was a guided book study of the text *Teaching and Learning Excellence: Engaging Self and Others with Emotional Intelligence* (Nelson et al., 2015) with interactive lessons to help the participants understand the topic. We also offered a Zoom conference call each week where participants could join a focus group discussion with myself, Dr. Low, and Dr. Hammett, which are two of the authors of the text. Participants took a self-assessment called the *Skills for Career And Life Effectiveness*, or SCALE assessment (Nelson & Low, 2019) to appraise their personal transformative emotional intelligence (TEI) skills before the book study began and at the end of the book study. The self-reflective conversations during the conference calls showed that the participants were not only developing their self-awareness but, also, becoming more aware of their interactions with peers, administrators, in their personal relationships, and with students. Just helping them to become more aware of their TEI skills seemed to have an immediate impact on their interpersonal skills of assertion, anxiety control, anger control, and empathy. Even if the educators did not choose to implement all of the learning from the study, we theorized that it would be difficult for them to unknow what they learned and that new learning would have a positive effect on their relationships with students, fellow educators, and families. This theory seemed to be validated based on the stories related from the participants during the last few focus group meetings.

The second part of the project included guided coaching from me based on the SCALE completed by each educator as the first step in helping them develop their personal TEI skills. Because coaching and TEI should be self-directed the participants were invited to select one skill they wanted to develop. Through the Zoom calls and personal communication the participants identified their chosen skill, created an action plan for development, identified metrics to know whether it was accomplished, and what to do next for additional skill development.

The third part of the study was dedicated to training teachers to embed SEL Learning Standards into their lesson plans. Having a new lens for looking at their lessons and new understanding and appreciation on how to develop SEL skills while teaching would make implementation less arduous; less about one more thing on my plate, and more natural; more about how I can be integrative, and more affective and meaningful in my teaching and learning. Some of the districts already had an SEL program they were using. I would like to propose that the type of program being used is not as important as knowing how to implement it. In this study the focus was using the SEL program already district approved and embedding that learning into the content lesson plan. What surprised me the most was the difficulty teachers had embedding additional learning. It would have been my thought that most teachers use various instructional strategies throughout their lessons so embedding SEL content into what they are already doing would not be difficult. What was found is that teachers were unable to view their lessons from the perspective of SEL skills. This observation points to the need for additional training through preservice, professional development, and classroom support.

The fourth part of the study was specific training on the collection and analysis of student achievement data, intervention planning, and instructional design for accountability (see the Every Student Succeeds Act). Similar to the challenges descried by teacher participants when trying to embed SEL content into lessons, the data collection and analysis was difficult for teachers to accomplish. I feel it would be easier for teachers if they were more confident about embedding SEL and had a better understanding of what interventions could look like, more training and practice using those interventions, and more experience with the data collection piece. It was during this part of the study that it became apparent how this kind of training could best serve educators moving forward.

I had written a university semester course that mirrored the study with approximately four weeks being devoted to each of the components: book study, skills development, embedded lessons, and data collection on interventions. However, based on initial takeaways from this study I think pre-service education should have a minimum of two semester long courses; one course to learn about TEI and how to develop personal skills and one course to learn about the implementation of intervention strategies in lessons, including collecting and analyzing data. Having two separate courses would allow additional time for participants to develop the self-awareness skills and subsequent TEI strengths that naturally evolve. This personally meaningful growth process was very evident from the focus group interviews conducted during this study. A separate course for student development provides the training needed to understand and practice how to look at all we do as educators through the lens of SEL/TEI, create meaningful interventions or implement a district approved program, and collect data to drive instruction and supports for both students and educators. As an alternative, a 15-hour certificate program would devote one entire course to each of the four phases, and a fifth practicum course offered to provide teacher participants the opportunity to have either synchronous or asynchronous TEI integration coaching using technology.

    I believe this study will be significant for several reasons. First, there is ample research to support the need to develop emotional intelligence in adults. Strong emotional intelligence skills are linked to happier and healthier lives. If EI skills are important in life for adults, then they are certainly important in life for public school children, too. Beginning this development early in life can have a profound effect on coping mechanisms, relationship skills, academic performance, job success, and overall happiness. There is also research that reports the positive relationship between a teacher and student as a key factor in academic achievement. By developing the emotional intelligence skills of both teachers and students the relationship factors are enhanced tremendously. Additionally, teachers can be better prepared to manage the needs and behaviors of their students, a satisfaction factor that will reduce the number of teachers leaving the profession. Including this type of comprehensive training in educator preparation programs and follow-on professional development is a necessary addition to support all education professionals.

Reform Student Supports for Mental Health and Behavior

I have worked with many schools and districts planning for additional personnel for discipline support. I offer the challenge to redirect the efforts from having enough personnel to handle the discipline needs of the school to having the personnel to support students differently, so the discipline incidents are reduced. I am also aware that most discipline support is provided at the secondary level since that is where there may be a greater instance. However, mental health and behavior issues or disorders do not begin in adolescents or adulthood without starting in childhood and early childhood.

I would open the conversation to include a different support structure that is not top heavy in secondary education, rather bottom heavy in the primary grades, especially in the pre-K through second grade levels. There is so much brain development happening through these developmental years I think that much of the intervention efforts would be of greater benefit for students' quality of life and change the educational success trajectory for those who are most in need. These changes could reduce drop-out rates, school violence, self-harm and suicide, and positively impact academic achievement, job satisfaction, and school culture.

Reform Discipline Supports for Mental Health and Behavior

An important area to open a dialogue is disciplinary practices. Some studies are being done that correlate psychological distress and exclusionary practices (Ford et al., 2017). Other studies support alternatives to removing students from the educational setting. "The damaging long-lasting effects of 'zero tolerance' has gotten more attention over the past few years, sparking a movement among many schools to move away from these practices and focus more on social-emotional learning, restorative practices, and positive behavioral interventions" (Luster, 2018). It is important to create equitable discipline with restorative practices; done right. The main problem with most school reform efforts is the *all-or-nothing* and *one-size-fits-all* practices. However, these are not the only issues with reforming practices. Adopting the new methods without fully implementing the prevention and intervention strategies leaves the program flat and unable to realize the full benefit (Walker, 2020). There needs to be a *whole-system* approach to school reform like the system proposed by Vincent et al. (2016) Their School-wide Positive and Restorative Discipline (SWPRD) program blends school-wide positive behavior interventions and supports with restorative practices to promote positive classroom relationships (Vincent et al., 2016). Preliminary results of their pilot program have been very positive and may be further supported by Hattie's influencing factors and the significance of relationships on educational outcomes (Hattie, 2017).

Reform School Safety Plans for Mental Health and Behavior Awareness and Proactive Strategies

Safety plans are another area of focus for campus and district conversations in relation to mental health and behavior in schools. Safety plan consideration for the physical and mental wellbeing of every student and all personnel should be paramount with funding and staffing adequate to manage emergency planning and responses. Again, this point is where I stress the need to have a strong support in lower grades to promote positive behavior and mental health support as a preemptive measure in the safety plan as opposed to just a crisis reaction. The more and better proactive measures that are put into place, the fewer responses and reactions will need to be taken.

Educational leaders should reverse engineer the safety plan the same way we unpack educational standards for vertical and horizontal planning. Beginning with the mental health issues and behaviors seen in high school, what planning needs to be put in place to train and condition students through SEL to have better outcomes? What type of training needs to happen with the teachers to be more prepared to identify and respond appropriately to mental health issues? What kind of thinking and TEI skills need to be taught to teachers to engender better behavior outcomes for all students?

Talk About it!

As mentioned in the introduction, this book was not written as an immediate answer to the mental health and behavior crises we are seeing worldwide. This book is meant to provide an invitation for dialogue on the school reforms needed to appropriately educate, support, and launch students into adulthood with the social-emotional skills needed to successfully engage with life. Avoiding a *one-size-fits-all* approach to education and using the *Davis Behavior Support Model* to couch reform conversations is a good place to start. The purpose of those conversations should focus on strategic, intentional design architectures that your school or district needs to properly support teachers, administrators, students, families, and the community in both mental health and behavior development needs. From this starting place, schools can design and implement integrated plans to provide a more meaningful education for all students, a more joyful and fulfilling work experience for educators, and help develop productive, self-evident, and independent adults for generations to come. I have but one last question for you to consider: Can we talk?

References

American Academy of Child and Adolescent Psychiatry. (2018). *Conduct Disorder*. https://www.aacap.org/aacap/families_and_youth/facts_for_families/fff-guide/conduct-disorder-033.aspx

American Academy of Child and Adolescent Psychiatry. (2019). *Oppositional Defiant Disorder*. AACAP. https://www.aacap.org/aacap/families_and_youth/facts_for_families/fff-guide/Children-With-Oppositional-Defiant-Disorder-072.aspx

American Psychiatric Association. (2013). *Diagnostic and Statistical Manual of Mental Disorders* (5th ed.). American Psychiatric Association.

Beckmann, J., & Heckhausen, H. (2018). Situational Determinants of Behavior. In J. Heckhausen & H. Heckhausen (Eds.), *Motivation and Action* (pp. 113–162). Springer International Publishing. https://doi.org/10.1007/978-3-319-65094-4_4

Bolier, L., Haverman, M., Westerhof, G. J., Riper, H., Smit, F., & Bohlmeijer, E. (2013). Positive psychology interventions: A meta-analysis of randomized controlled studies. *BMC Public Health*, *13*(1), 119. https://doi.org/10.1186/1471-2458-13-119

Carver-Thomas, D., & Darling-Hammond, L. (2017). Teacher turnover: Why It matters and what we can do about it. *Learning Policy Institute*. https://learningpolicyinstitute.org/product/teacher-turnover

Child Mind Institute. (2016). *2016 Child Mind Institute Children's Mental Health Report*. https://childmind.org/report/2016-childrens-mental-health-report/

Coulombe, J. A., Reid, G. J., Boyle, M. H., & Racine, Y. (2011). Sleep problems, tiredness, and psychological symptoms among healthy adolescents. *Journal of Pediatric Psychology, 36*(1), 25–35. https://doi.org/10.1093/jpepsy/jsq028

Curby, T. W., Brown, C. A., Bassett, H. H., & Denham, S. A. (2015). Associations between preschoolers' social-emotional competence and preliteracy skills: Social-emotional competence and preliteracy. *Infant and Child Development, 24*(5), 549–570. https://doi.org/10.1002/icd.1899

Danielson, M. L., Bitsko, R. H., Ghandour, R. M., Holbrook, J. R., Kogan, M. D., & Blumberg, S. J. (2018). Prevalence of parent-reported ADHD diagnosis and associated treatment among U.S. children and adolescents, 2016. *Journal of Clinical Child & Adolescent Psychology, 47*(2), 199–212. https://www.tandfonline.com/doi/abs/10.1080/15374416.2017.1417860

Davis, K. K. (2019a). *Determining Impact of Appreciative Inquiry: A Case Study - ProQuest*. https://search.proquest.com/openview/f818fb43abdd1d0eaf35b72364518bc1/1?pq-origsite=gscholar&cbl=18750&diss=y

Davis, K. K. (2019b). Exploring best practices among appreciative inquiry practitioners for determining impact. *AI Practitioner*, *21*(3), 66–91. https://doi.org/dx.doi.org/10.12781/978-1-907549-40-3-12

Epstein, S. (1991). Cognitive-experiential self theory: Implications for developmental psychology. In *Self processes and development* (pp. 79–123). Lawrence Erlbaum Associates, Inc.

ESSA Mental and Behavioral Health Services for School Psychologists. (2019). National Association of School Psychologists (NASP). https://www.nasponline.org/research-and-policy/policy-priorities/relevant-law/the-every-student-succeeds-act/essa-implementation-resources/essa-mental-and-behavioral-health-services-for-school-psychologists

EthosHealth. (2017). How does hunger impact your children's learning? *EthosHealth*. http://www.ethoshealth.com.au/blog1/how-does-hunger-impact-your-children-s-learning

Ford, T. J., Parker, C., Salim, J., Goodman, R., & Henley, W. (2017). The relationship between exclusion from school and mental health: A secondary analysis of the British Child and Adolescent Mental Health Surveys 2004 and 2007. *Psychological Medicine*. https://ore.exeter.ac.uk/repository/bitstream/handle/10871/28337/Psychological%20medicine%20revision%2023%20June%202017.pdf?sequence=1

Gonzalez-Roma, V., Schaufeli, W. B., Bakker, A. B., & Lloret, S. (2006). Burnout and work engagement: Independent factors or opposite poles? *Journal of Vocational Behavior*, *68*, 165–174. https://www.sciencedirect.com/science/article/abs/pii/S0001879105000229

Grant, S., Hamilton, L., Wrabel, S., Gomez, C., Whitaker, A., Leschitz, J., Unlu, F., Chavez-Herrerias, E., Baker, G., Barrett, M., Harris, M., & Ramos, A. (2017). *Social and Emotional Learning Interventions Under the Every Student Succeeds Act: Evidence Review*. RAND Corporation. https://doi.org/10.7249/RR2133

Grant, Sean, Hamilton, L., Wrabel, S., Gomez, C., Whitaker, A., Leschitz, J., Unlu, F., Chavez-Herrerias, E., Baker, G., Barrett, M., Harris, M., & Ramos, A. (2017). *How the Every Student Succeeds Act Can Support Social and Emotional Learning*. RAND Corporation. https://doi.org/10.7249/RB9988

Haidt, J., & Paresky, P. (2019). By mollycoddlling our children, we're fuelling mental illness in teenagers. *The Guardian*.

Hattie, J. (2017). *Visible Learning Plus: 250+ Influences on Student Achievement*. https://visible-learning.org/wp-content/uploads/2018/03/VLPLUS-252-Influences-Hattie-ranking-DEC-2017.pdf

Hupp, S. D., Reitman, D., & Jewell, J. D. (2008). Cognitive-Behavioral Theory. In *Handbook of clinical psychology* (Vol. 2, pp. 263–283).

Hutton, J. S., Dudley, J., Horowitz-Kraus, T., DeWitt, T., & Holland, S. K. (2019). Associations between screen-based media use and brain white matter integrity in preschool-aged children. *JAMA Pediatrics*, e193869–e193869. https://doi.org/10.1001/jamapediatrics.2019.3869

Kolbe, L. J., Allensworth, D. D., Potts-Datema, W., & White, D. R. (2015). What Have We Learned From Collaborative Partnerships to Concomitantly Improve Both Education and Health? *Journal of School Health*, *85*(11), 766–774. https://doi.org/10.1111/josh.12312

Krueger, R. F. (1999). The structure of common mental disorders. *Archives of General Psychiatry*, *56*(10), 921–926. https://doi.org/10.1001/archpsyc.56.10.921

Leibenluft, E. (2017). Irritability in children: What we know and what we need to learn. *World Psychiatry*, *16*(1), 100–101. https://doi.org/10.1002/wps.20397

Linke, J., Stavish, C., Clayton, M., Kircanski, K., Benson, B., Brotman, M. A., Leibenluft, E., Winkler, A., & Pine, D. (2020). Connectivity Guided Dimensions of Psychopathology in Youth. *Biological Psychiatry*, *87*(9), S114. https://doi.org/10.1016/j.biopsych.2020.02.312

Liu, H., Atrooz, F., Salvi, A., & Salim, S. (2017). Behavioral and cognitive impact of early life stress: Insights from an animal model. *Progress in Neuro-Psychopharmacology and Biological Psychiatry*, *78*, 88–95. https://doi.org/10.1016/j.pnpbp.2017.05.015

Luster, S. (2018). *How Exclusionary Discipline Creates Disconnected Students*. NEA Today. http://neatoday.org/2018/07/19/how-exclusionary-discipline-creates-disconnected-students/

Maslach, C., Schaufeli, W. B., & Leiter, M. P. (2001). Job burnout. *Annual Review of Psychology*, *52*, 397.

Mayo Clinic. (2020). *Attention-deficit/hyperactivity disorder (ADHD) in children—Symptoms and causes*. Mayo Clinic. https://www.mayoclinic.org/diseases-conditions/adhd/symptoms-causes/syc-20350889

McCarthy, C. (2017). *4 ways to help your child get enough sleep*. Harvard Health Blog. https://www.health.harvard.edu/blog/four-ways-to-help-your-child-get-enough-sleep-2017092612472

Mental Health Challenges. (n.d.). [Mental Health Non-Profit]. The Main Place. http://www.themainplace.org/mentalchallenges.html

Mental health disorders in adolescents. Committee Opinion No. 75. American College of Obstetricians and Gynecologists. (2017). *Obstet Gynecol*, *130*, e32-41. https://www.acog.org/Clinical-Guidance-and-Publications/Committee-Opinions/Committee-on-Adolescent-Health-Care/Mental-Health-Disorders-in-Adolescents?IsMobileSet=false

Mental Health First Aid USA. (2020). Mental Health First Aid. https://www.mentalhealthfirstaid.org/

Merikangas, K. R., Nakamura, E. F., & Kessler, R. C. (2009). Epidemiology of mental disorders in children and adolescents. *Dialogues in Clinical Neuroscience, 11*(1), 7–20. https://www.ncbi.nlm.nih.gov/pmc/articles/PMC2807642/

Merk Manuals. (2020). *Temper Tantrums—Children's Health Issues.* Merck Manuals Consumer Version. https://www.merckmanuals.com/home/children-s-health-issues/behavioral-problems-in-children/temper-tantrums

Munzer, T. G., Miller, A. L., Weeks, H. M., Kaciroti, N., & Radesky, J. (2019). Parent-toddler social reciprocity during reading from electronic tablets vs print books. *JAMA Pediatrics, 173*(11), 1076–1083. https://doi.org/10.1001/jamapediatrics.2019.3480

National Center for Learning Disabilities. (2019). *What is Response to Intervention (RTI)?* RTI Network. http://www.rtinetwork.org/learn/what/whatisrti

National Council for Behavioral Health. (2016). *Mental Health First Aid for Adults Assisting Young People.*

National Council for Behavioral Health. https://www.thenationalcouncil.org/

Nelson, D. B., & Low, G. R. (2019). *The SCALE®—Skills for Career And Life Effectiveness*. The Skills for Career and Life Effectiveness Assessment. https://doscale.com/

Nelson, D. B., Low, G. R., Nelson, K. W., & Hammett, R. D. (2015). *Teaching and learning excellence: Engaging self and others with emotional intelligence*. Emotional Intelligence Learning Systems.

Nobel, E., Hoekstra, P. J., Agnes Brunnekreef, J., Messink-de Vries, D. E. H., Fischer, B., Emmelkamp, P. M. G., & van den Hoofdakker, B. J. (2020). Home-based parent training for school-aged children with attention-deficit/hyperactivity disorder and behavior problems with remaining impairing disruptive behaviors after routine treatment: A randomized controlled trial. *European Child & Adolescent Psychiatry*, *29*(3), 395–408. https://doi.org/10.1007/s00787-019-01375-9

O'Connor, M., & Cameron, G. (2017). The Geelong Grammar Positive Psychology Experience. In E. Frydenberg, A. J. Martin, & R. J. Collie (Eds.), *Social and Emotional Learning in Australia and the Asia-Pacific: Perspectives, Programs and Approaches* (pp. 353–370). Springer. https://doi.org/10.1007/978-981-10-3394-0_19

PBIS.org | School-Wide. (2019). https://www.pbis.org/topics/school-wide

Perrone, F., Player, D., & Youngs, P. (2019). Administrative climate, early career teacher burnout, and turnover. *Journal of School Leadership*, *29*(3), 191–209. https://doi.org/10.1177/1052684619836823

Rumschlag, K. E. (2017). Teacher burnout: A quantitative analysis of emotional exhaustion, personal accomplishment, and depersonalization. *International Management Review*, *13*(1), 15. https://pdfs.semanticscholar.org/aa58/0caa8ad6596b82a21698a96786ccfbeb2671.pdf

Seligman, M. E. P., Ernst, R. M., Gillham, J., Reivich, K., & Linkins, M. (2009). Positive education: Positive psychology and classroom interventions. *Oxford Review of Education*, *35*(3), 293–311. https://doi.org/10.1080/03054980902934563

Shabat-Simon, M., Shuster, A., Sela, T., & Levy, D. (2018). Objective physiological measurements but not subjective reports moderate the effect of hunger on choice behavior. *Frontiers in Psychology*, *9*. https://doi.org/10.3389/fpsyg.2018.00750

Shackleton, N., Bonell, C., Jamal, F., Allen, E., Mathiot, A., Elbourne, D., & Viner, R. (2019). Teacher burnout and contextual and compositional elements of school environment. *Journal of School Health*, *89*(12), 977–993. https://doi.org/10.1111/josh.12839

Situational Factors: Events in your Child's World Impacts Him. (2020). *The Center for Parenting Education.* https://centerforparentingeducation.org/library-of-articles/child-development/situational-factors/

Skaalvik, E. M., & Skaalvik, S. (2017). Dimensions of teacher burnout: Relations with potential stressors at school. *Social Psychology of Education, 20*(4), 775–790. https://doi.org/10.1007/s11218-017-9391-0

Vincent, C. G., Inglish, J., Girvan, E. J., Sprague, J. R., & McCabe, T. M. (2016). School-wide Positive and Restorative Discipline (SWPRD): Integrating School-wide Positive Behavior Interventions and Supports and Restorative Discipline. In R. J. Skiba, K. Mediratta, & M. K. Rausch (Eds.), *Inequality in School Discipline: Research and Practice to Reduce Disparities* (pp. 115–134). Palgrave Macmillan US. https://doi.org/10.1057/978-1-137-51257-4_7

Walker, T. (2020). *Restorative Practices in Schools Work... But They Can Work Better.* NEA Today. http://neatoday.org/2020/01/30/restorative-justice-in-schools-works/

Wertz, J., Zavos, H. M. S., Matthews, T., Gray, R., Best-Lane, J., Pariante, C. M., Moffitt, T. E., & Arseneault, L. (2016). Etiology of Pervasive versus situational antisocial behaviors: A multi-informant longitudinal cohort study. *Child Development, 87*(1), 312–325. https://doi.org/10.1111/cdev.12456

What Is Mental Illness? (2018). American Psychiatric Association. https://www.psychiatry.org/patients-families/what-is-mental-illness

Wheaton, A. G., Chapman, D. P., & Croft, J. B. (2016). School start times, sleep, behavioral, health, and academic outcomes: A review of the literature. *Journal of School Health, 86*(5), 363–381. https://doi.org/10.1111/josh.12388

Wichstrøm, L., Stenseng, F., Belsky, J., von Soest, T., & Hygen, B. W. (2019). Symptoms of internet gaming disorder in youth: Predictors and comorbidity. *Journal of Abnormal Child Psychology, 47*(1), 71–83. https://doi.org/10.1007/s10802-018-0422-x